The Road to Angkor

' … the mixture of trees and stones is so intricate … ' (*see p. 18*)

The Road to Angkor

Christopher Pym

JOHN BEAUFOY PUBLISHING

First published in 1959

This edition published in 2023 by
John Beaufoy Publishing Ltd.
in association with Edward Stanford Ltd.

John Beaufoy Publishing
11 Blenheim Court, 316 Woodstock Road, Oxford,
OX2 7NS, UK

ISBN 978-1-912081-32-5

Cover concept by Chris Jones
Designed and typeset by John Button, Gloucestershire, UK
Printed in India by Replika Press Pvt Ltd.

CONTENTS

FOUR: West from the Mekong

FIVE: The Road to Angkor

LIST OF ILLUSTRATIONS

All photographs by the author except No. 9
(Courtesy: Khmer Information Service)

ACKNOWLEDGEMENTS

This is not the place to thank those scholars who kindly fostered my interest in the ancient Khmer empire. I hope to thank them later on. Here I would like to express thanks to my family who helped and encouraged me (not forgetting Aunt Hester), and Mr. John Attenborough who did the same. I am also grateful to Mr. Anthony Cotel who made useful suggestions for improving this book.

It remains for me to thank a very large number of acquaintances in Indo-China who helped me to get to know the three countries of Laos, Cambodia and Viet-Nam. In particular I would like to thank my Cambodian teacher with whom I spent so many happy hours learning the Khmer language.

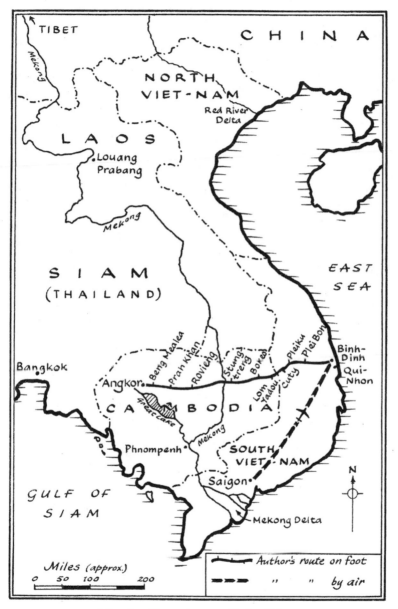

Map A – General map of Indo-China.

FOREWORD

On the 11 May, 1965, Mr Eric Ogden (Labour, Liverpool West Derby) rose to address the Commons on the subject of Christopher Pym, who had recently been fined a pound in the Cambridge Magistrates' Court for collecting money in the street. Pym, aged 36, married and with one child, was no panhandling layabout, as Ogden informed honourable members:

> His father was a chaplain of Trinity College, Cambridge, and his mother is a former Fellow of Girton College, Cambridge. He was educated at Marlborough, where he won an open exhibition to Cambridge, Trinity. He was a National Service officer and served with the British Intelligence Services in Cambodia ...

His grandfather had been Bishop of Bombay, his uncle Leslie Ruthven Pym was government whip under Churchill, and his cousin Francis, currently representing Cambridgeshire for the Conservatives, would one day lead the old squirearchy in their opposition to Margaret Thatcher. This branch of the family was Tory (there was a stately home called Hazells Hall), but Christopher was not. In 1960 he stood as an independent for the safe Labour seat of Blyth, then for Kent County Council, and at the 1964 General Election for Bristol South-East. All these were unsuccessful, although in Blyth he captured a respectable 9.5 per cent of the vote. In February 1965, and newly redundant, he rented premises in Saffron Walden, where another by-election was due:

As every hon. Member knows, contesting an election is an expensive business, and while Mr. Pym had money for his election address, which was in fact printed, he still required £150 to provide the necessary sum for his election deposit. The means that are often available to party members or party candidates were not available to an independent candidate. My Pym decided that he would try to raise £150 by collecting the money in the neighbouring towns of Colchester, Chelmsford, Bishops Stortford and Cambridge, believing that many people from the Saffron Walden constituency went into those towns. Unfortunately, as it proved, he went first to Cambridge.

Pym was arrested outside a Tesco on a Saturday morning in February 1965, an unwitting transgressor of numerous Acts regulating the collection of money from the public 'for the benefit of charitable or other purposes'. It was unacceptable, Mr Ogden said, that 'the ability of an honest and sincere man to stand for Parliament was reduced to an arid legal argument ... as to the precise interpretation of "or other purposes".' Nor did the trivial amount of Pym's fine matter, for a stain had been laid on his character. No doubt there should and would be changes to the law, and Mr Ogden therefore asked the Under-Secretary of the Home Department whether Christopher could be granted a Queen's Pardon.

But as the Joint Under-Secretary pointed out in reply, it had always been open to Pym to apply for a permit. 'I am limited by what the law allows and the discretion of my right hon. and learned Friend [the Home Secretary] is not such that he could intervene in this case.' The House adjourned, and presumably the fine remains on the record.

What are we to make of Christopher Pym, secret agent? Ogden's assertion that he worked for Intelligence in Cambodia seems hard to square with the innocence of *Road to Angkor* and its companion volume, *Mistapim in Cambodia*, in both of which Pym shows next to no interest in politics. His upper-middle class background and public school education would have made him a natural fit for Military Intelligence in Malaya, where he did his National Service, but in *Mistapim* he describes only his later position with an unspecified commercial company, and his description of his living arrangements sounds more Somerset Maugham than Graham Greene: 'everything was provided – car, house, garden, cook, gardener, cocktails, and so on'. By the end of 1954 his work in Malaya, whatever it was, was done, and he took a train to Bangkok. There he met a Thai prince who led him to Angkor, and amidst the temples he conceived the project which forms the subject of this book.

Angkor's empire stretched from the beaches of the South China Sea to the Three Pagodas Pass on the borders of Burma, and it was reasonable to suppose that it might have had highways. Four were already well known, running west, north-west, north-east and east, their remains easily recognisable today as broad earth embankments equipped with bridges, culverts, rest-houses and ponds (elephants need huge amounts of water), but the eastern one, which should have led to Vietnam, stopped well within Cambodia on the wrong side of the Mekong. Did it or did it not continue to the west bank, begin again on the far side (the ancient Khmers were master-engineers, but the Mekong would have been too much for them), and then up to the high plateau and down again to the sea? We now know it did not, but in Pym's day it was a perfectly valid question.

It seems unlikely that British Intelligence took much interest in ancient roads and kingdoms, and nor will the average modern reader, but fortunately *The Road to Angkor* is above all an adventure story. The time was propitious: the French had finally given up their attempt to hold on to their colonial empire by force, Vietnam was divided and Cambodia was at peace. There were tigers in the forests and obstructive officials in the towns, but with his rucksack on his back and rubber sandals on his feet, Christopher set off to find the road to Angkor.

There were two other items on his agenda. First was the question of whether he might find Stone Age axes and such: he did. Second, and more intriguing, was a 19th century Montagnard chieftain named Pim. The Montagnards were warriors, they spoke languages allied to those of Indonesia and lived in villages with spectacular longhouses; the Vietnamese called them *moi*, savages, and avoided them. One forms the impression that Pym's road was not much more than an excuse for his trip.

The reviewer for the Royal Geographical Society's *Geographical Journal* greeted the author of *The Road to Angkor* as 'a sympathetic and acute observer' and looked forward to 'the more serious work on Angkor and Khmer civilization which he hopes to publish "in thirty year's time or longer if need be"'. 1966 saw an abridged edition of Henri Mouhot's account of his travels in Siam, Cambodia and Laos, the first reprinting in English of this important work in over a century, and in 1968 *The Ancient Civilization of Angkor* appeared, ground-breaking for concentrating on the lives of ordinary people rather than the deeds of kings. And that was all. *Mistapim in Cambodia* mentions a novel, apparently about a romance between a foreigner and a Cambodian girl, but it was never published – perhaps someone, someday, will find the manuscript – but a decade after his return from Cambodia, Pym was no longer a traveller.

Instead there was the pursuit of quixotic politics as an under-funded if respected independent. From 1975 he worked for the Open University, for which he did innovative work on renew-able energy and children with special needs. From 1983 he was a councillor for Milton Keynes, campaigning for community areas and community housing (a distant echo of the Montagnard long-houses?) and for play areas and a council-funded play-officer. He was 'the best mayor Milton Keynes never had' (the quote comes from Pym's obituary in the *Independent*, written by Hugh Ruthven, who, one suspects, might be Hugh Ruthven Pym, health editor for the BBC and Christopher Pym's nephew), and 'he was particularly proud to be elected the first chair of governors at a new Milton Keynes school, Walton High'. Pym was an asset to his community, but one cannot help wondering what might have been had he chosen the path of a Jan Morris or a Gavin Young, contemporaries whose lives tracked his up to a certain point.

Could Pym's 1957 journey be done today? The border is open, the road is good and Westerners have been sighted striding along it, but it would not be the same. The forests, victims of the logging industry, are going or gone, and Norman Lewis, in the preface to the 1982 edition of his *A Dragon Apparent*, sketches the fate of Pim's people in the war that was about to come to Vietnam:

> The longhouses ... were bombed to nothingness by the B52s in the Vietnam war, and such of the population who survived were forced into the armies fighting the nationalist Viet Cong, who were revenged on them in due course when the US aban-donment of the country took place.

Today Vietnamese settlers are filling the highlands. On the Cambodian side the tribal people are still a majority, but traditional lifestyles are eroding under the pressure of modernisation. Angkor is one of the world's top destinations, and although the immense site of Preah Khan of Kampong Svay, where the road begins and ends, remains comparatively unvisited, the Cambodian government would like to attract more tourists.

Philip Coggan

INTRODUCTION

Angkor is the ancient capital of the Khmer empire, a fabulous city of ruins buried deep in the jungles of Cambodia. In the autumn of 1954 I was touring South-East Asia and determined to visit Angkor, though it might be 'see Angkor and die', perhaps, for the war in French Indo-China was barely over. I started by rail from Malaya, and at Bangkok, the Thai capital, I heard news that the land frontier between Thailand and Cambodia had just been re-opened. Within a few days I joined a small party of tourists led by a Siamese Prince, and together we drove to see the strangest city of ruins which man has ever witnessed. The most striking of Angkor's ruins are Angkor the Great, a walled city with five enormous gateways, and Angkor Wat, a huge temple with five towers which soar majestically above the surrounding forest. 'Perhaps it might be compared', wrote one visitor, 'to the impression that would be produced on a wanderer in another millennium coming suddenly upon the ruins of Manhattan rising silent and empty above the Hudson.'[1]

The most astonishing thing about Angkor is the size of the ruined buildings, and the way in which many of them are still locked in the clasp of giant rain-trees with orchids trailing above the sculptures and monkeys swinging from darkness into sunlight through the deserted galleries. For Angkor was once the 'lost city' *par excellence,* and some of its temples are still hard to reach and enter. Fallen sculptures block the doorways. Lintels have slipped sideways, exposing crevices which branches of tropical trees have clawed wider and deeper, till now the mixture

1   Benjamin Rowland, *The Art and Architecture of India.*

of trees and stone is so intricate that the doorways are hardly distinguishable. The jungle reclaims its lost ground so quickly that Angkor's curators can barely hold it in check, though the most important temples, like Angkor Wat, are clear of rubble and open to tourists. Elsewhere, on the walls of Angkor the Great, for example, you must take a weapon to clear a way through the luscious creepers and plants which choke the winding path over the ruins. In some unrestored temples the seeds of rain-trees have planted themselves in the most unlikely places – on the tops of crumbling towers or in the chasms of cracked walls. Here the trees have taken root, and spring skywards as if they thrived on the very stone which imprisons their roots.

Wherever you wander among the ruins, you find the statues of gods, Siva and Vishnu from the Hindu pantheon, and the god who, for the ancient Khmers, eventually displaced them all – Buddha. It is the smiling face of Buddha, in his incarnation as Lokesvara, the 'Healer', which looks down from above the five gateways of Angkor the Great. In the centre of the ruined city there is an extraordinary temple called the Bayon, made entirely of these smiling Buddha-faces; at least that is what you think when you see it for the first time. In reality it is composed of a series of towers, each one sculptured on all four sides with the same smiling face.

> 'These towers [wrote a French traveller] might have been compared in outline to colossal pineapples placed on end ... high in the air, those quadruple faces gazed at the four cardinal points, gazed everywhere, with the same drooping eyelids, the same expression of ironical pity, the same smile. They affirmed, they repeated until it became a kind of obsession, the omnipresence of the god of Angkor'.[2]

2   Pierre Loti, *Le Pèlerin D'Angkor.*

So on this first visit in 1954 I was just one more tourist who succumbed to the magic of Angkor's ruins in the forest and the mysterious smile of her omnipresent god. During much of the next three years, at first in London and Paris, then in Cambodia, I studied the Khmers, and, in 1957 made the journey described in this book. The civilization of the ancient Khmers is no longer a mystery, but Angkor with its great temples still exercises a mysterious fascination which I can no better explain than can those many others who have once passed beneath its spell. Though the journey described here originated in an interest and sympathy for the ancient Khmers, the road to Angkor took me through a modern country whose god is still the smiling Buddha, and whose people are descended direct from the builders of Angkor the Great. These people, gay, kind and hospitable, are the modern Cambodians. It was in their company that I travelled much of *The Road to Angkor*.

Besides being interested in the ancient Khmers, I began to learn about the ancient Chams, who lived in a kingdom called Champa which has now disappeared. The ancient Khmer empire was at its height between the ninth and thirteenth centuries A.D. The Chams rivalled the Khmers and fought many wars with them. Both Khmers and Chams were Hinduized peoples, and their cultures flowered as the result of intermarriage between Hindu settlers from India and the indigenous tribes of the Indo-China peninsula. These tribesmen – that is what I call them, though the French call them *montagnards* (highlanders) – are a great number of peoples who have lived in Indo-China since long before Khmers or Chams emerged. They are still living in the hills of Indo-China today, though they have no political autonomy.

From the fourteenth century onwards the ancient Khmer kingdom became weaker and weaker, till in the second half of the nineteenth century the French saved it from giving in to its warlike neighbours, the Siamese in the west, and the Viet-Namese in the east. The Chams had already given in to the Annamites (old name for Viet-Namese) who came from the north and expelled them from their old territory along the coast of the China Sea. Cham buildings were not on the same scale as the Khmer temples, and it is strange that Marco Polo should have known Champa but not Angkor. The rediscovery of these two ancient kingdoms took place in the latter part of the nineteenth century. Angkor was dramatically rediscovered in 1860 by the French naturalist and explorer Henri Mouhot, who was led to the threshold of Angkor Wat by missionaries and exclaimed to his companions: 'It is grander than anything left us by Greece or Rome.' The Cham ruins, mostly brick towers, were found near the sea. The French took some of the best Khmer and Cham sculpture home to France, where it can be seen today in the Musée Guimet, Paris, but eighty tons of Cham statues were lost when the packet-boat carrying them was shipwrecked in the Red Sea in 1886. Survivors of the Cham people still live today as forgotten minorities, some in South Viet-Nam; others in Cambodia. The Khmers have survived in their own country, Cambodia, and in this book 'Khmer' and 'Cambodian' mean the same thing, whether they refer to the people, the civilization, or the language.

I have been referring to Indo-China, but in theory Indo-China no longer exists, and, since no better term is available, *The Times* newspaper has been reduced to dubbing this part of the world 'what we used to call Indo-China'. It is occupied today by hundreds of peoples, some independent, and some not. The picture is confused because several of these peoples have recently changed their names and the names of their countries since the French left Indo-China in 1954. For example, what we learnt at school as Tanking is now part of North Viet-Nam, and Cochin-China is part of South Viet-Nam. There has never been an 'Indo-Chinese' people, just as there has never been a country called 'Anglo-Gallica'. Indo-China was so called because the origin of her peoples is partly 'Indo-' (e.g. Cambodia) and partly 'China' (e.g. Viet-Nam). Though the war in Indo-China is now only a forgotten headline, many people remember the disaster of Dien-Bien-Phu, after which an armistice was signed and France lost for good her former possessions – Cambodia, Laos, Annam, Tonking, and Cochin-China. The last three of these became the new state of Viet-Nam, which had fought for independence since 1945.

An agreement guaranteeing the peace of Indo-China was signed at Geneva in 1954. Viet-Nam became a divided state. The north was kept by the Viet-Minh Communists, whose leader has long been Ho Chi Minh, a Europe-trained Communist, known affectionately to his followers and enemies as 'Uncle Ho'. South Viet-Nam became a separate anti-Communist state led by a pro-American Roman Catholic, Ngo Dinh Diem. His palace is in Saigon, a city well known to readers of Graham Greene's book *The Quiet American*. Bombs were being thrown when Greene was there during the war. They were still being thrown when I passed through in 1957, three years after the Geneva agreement.

Cambodia was the only country of the three to hold elections at once and fulfil the conditions of the Geneva agreement. Her king, known to many Europeans as the 'jazz-composing King of Cambodia', abdicated the throne, formed a political party and won every seat in both the 1955 and the 1958 elections. His father was crowned king in his stead. The coronation was held with great pomp in 1956, and the ex-king, Prince Sihanouk, played his saxophone for the amusement of honoured foreign guests. Since then the ex-king has been Prime Minister several times, and secured important aid for Cambodia by judicious visits to Communist and non-Communist countries. At the time of my journey these countries were trying to woo Cambodia from her avowed policy of neutrality, formulated by Prince Sihanouk. This certainly seemed a wise policy for a young recently independent country, but it led to inevitable difficulties with Cambodia's anti-Communist neighbour, South Viet-Nam.

Laos remained divided like Viet-Nam, till in 1958 the pro-Communist faction, previously known as Pathet Lao, led by a Prince of royal blood, integrated itself with the non-Communist faction, led by another Prince of royal blood. Viet-Minh Communists were still at large within her frontiers when I made my journey, and they sometimes crossed into the neighbouring countries of Cambodia and South Viet-Nam.

My journey on the road to Angkor took me to South Viet-Nam and Cambodia, but not to Laos or North Viet-Nam. Its starting-point, as the reader will see from the next chapter, was Binh-Dinh in South Viet-Nam, on the coast of the China Sea.

ONE

Hills and Tribes

CHAPTER ONE

REASONS WHY

The main purpose of my journey was to seek traces of a twelfth-century Khmer road which once linked Angkor with the capital of Champa. The existence of this road has been known for a long time, and, as well as being mentioned in an inscription, parts of it have been traced on the ground. These are listed in the Inventory of Ancient Khmer Monuments compiled by a French infantry officer at the beginning of this century. Later investigators have traced the road from Angkor to a point about eighty miles east – as far as the temple of Prah Khan in the sparsely populated forests of north Cambodia. According to the inscription, there were fifty-seven rest-houses on the road to Champa, some of which have been found in ruins between Angkor and the temple of Prah Khan. None, so far as I knew, had been found between Prah Khan and the coast. Champa had two capitals, north and south, and it is not even certain to which of these capitals the road led. I chose the northern capital near Binh-Dinh as my starting-point – an arbitrary choice, for I might well have chosen the southern capital. If a new Khmer rest-house could be found in either of these regions the existence of the ancient Khmer road to the coast would be proved. That is what I hoped to do, and I began by studying the geography of Indo-China as a whole.

There are mountains in the north and centre – that is Laos. There is a plain flooded annually by a river in the south – that is Cambodia. To the east of the plain there is a plateau – this is where the tribesmen live, though they also live in the mountains. East of the plateau there is a long coastal plain, which the Chams once inhabited and where my starting-point, Binh-Dinh, lay near to the coast. My zone of research was limited by the position of passes up to the plateau from Binh-Dinh, the most obvious of which was the *Col d'Ankhé*. Beyond the plateau I would come to the River Mekong, which rises in Tibet, flows through the mountains of Laos, over the Cambodian plain and out to sea by a river-delta in South Viet-Nam – a huge river, more than half the length of the Amazon and ten times longer than the Thames.

A secondary purpose of the journey was to look for Neolithic tools in an area on the plateau west of Pleiku. Finds at a plantation near Pleiku, and farther north, make scholars think that a Neolithic culture once spread far across the plateau. Anything I found would tend to confirm this thesis. The Neolithic period in Indo-China is less clearly defined than the Khmer and Cham civilizations which followed it. Its tools consist mostly of stone axe-heads, known in several countries of South-East Asia as 'thunder-axes'.

I had a third, and less serious, objective, which suggested itself when I was reading some French explorers' accounts of tribes on the plateau. One of them mentioned a chieftain called 'Pim', my namesake, whom he described as 'young, handsome, brave, quick, eloquent and confident in the future'. The explorer says that Pim went out with his bow and arrow and shot something for dinner. Then there was dancing, which the French found *un peu grossièrement lascive, so* their leader suggested a war-dance, an odd thing to do, since the dance was never performed except on the eve of real war, which Pim was trying to avoid. Later they looked at the family riches, jars, worth twenty slaves each, and gongs, of which Pim was particularly proud and fond. In 1888 another Frenchman visited Pim's village. This was Mayréna, who made himself king of all the tribes in the region and took the title of 'Marie the First'. He was an unsuccessful version of the Englishman who founded a dynasty in Borneo and called himself the 'Rajah Brooke'. King Marie persuaded some missionaries to help him under the pretext of annexing the tribal areas to France. In fact, he claimed that his tribesmen were an independent people. In one of their letters to him, the French had referred to chieftain Pim as 'independent'. Marie argued that if Pim was independent, therefore independence was beyond question for all the country which stretched from the villages of Pim to the River Mekong. The arguments which King Marie used to discourage the French from meddling with his tribes sound curiously modern in the context of today, when these tribesmen, descendants of Pim, are being colonized by the Viet-Namese. Since my journey would take me through 'Pim' country, I decided it would be amusing to look for Phu's village, introduce myself to his, descendants if they could be found, and see if they had any views on independence, that is independence, not from the French, but from their new overlords, the Viet-Namese. All this had nothing to do with the ancient Khmer road, but promised to be an entertaining sidetrack.

I now had to decide *how* I would make the journey. Before the war, there was a motorable road (No. 9) which linked Binh-Dinh with Cambodia, but it had fallen into decay. In any case, I had no suitable vehicle, so I took the decision to walk. I would have preferred horses or elephants like the early explorers, for in this way seven hours on foot can be reduced to three in the saddle, but my resources would run to none of these luxuries. I wondered if anyone had ever *walked* from the coast to the River Mekong. I daresay many Frenchmen were obliged to do it during

27

the war, and certainly in the time of Angkor many Khmer and Cham soldiers would have tramped the weary road to Champa and back. There was also the great Khmer king, Jayavarman the Seventh, builder of the Bayon, who returned from Champa across the plateau when his throne was usurped at Angkor. In the sixteenth century two Portuguese adventurers made their way from the coast over the mountains to Laos. Their adventures are splendidly described in Alan Houghton Brodrick's book *Little Vehicle,* in which he adds by way of comment on their achievement that to do this even today would be something of an adventure.

CHAPTER TWO

SAIGON

My story of the journey, based on a diary, begins in Saigon, the capital of South Viet-Nam. I arrived there by an aeroplane of Air Vietnam. Cambodia and Laos also have their own civil airlines now. Within a few hours of my arrival, but not, I believe, as a result of it, plastic bombs began exploding, and the streets burgeoned with police. As I have hinted already, the atmosphere was that of *The Quiet American,* with the added excitement that students from minor universities in the U.S.A. are now preparing theses on 'Greene's Saigon', rather like 'Joyce's Dublin'. They wander round cafés, trying to find places where Graham Greene once had a drink. Instead, they find places where Michael Redgrave ate an omelette. For Saigon is best known to the Americans, and ourselves I suppose, from the film *The Quiet American,* which bears as little relation to the book as an omelette to a Pernod.

One day was meant to suffice for making arrangements in Saigon, but I did not know what formalities needed attention. The British Embassy seemed a likely place to find out. I saw someone who had just arrived and knew 'almost nothing'. Later I tried the British Information Centre and met an efficient girl who did not know where Binh-Dinh was and complained about being 'stuck in Saigon'. It seemed a pity that British representatives abroad did not have more chance to see the countries in which they were serving.

The Viet-Namese Institute of Historical Research helped solve the map problem. I compared my own notes with their large-scale maps and found that villages would be frequent on the coastal plain, but seemed to thin out across the plateau. I found Pim's village, or so I thought, for it had the right name, Plei Bon, and lay about sixty kilometres west of the *Col d'Ankhé* pass and about forty east of Pleiku. It appeared to be divided in half, west and east of a marshy stream. There was still time to visit the National School of Administration, where I hoped to find a French-speaking student from Pim's tribe, the Bahnars, who could give me advice about 'dos' and 'don'ts' in the tribal areas. It turned out that other tribes were sending students to the School, but not the Bahnars of Plei Bon.

There are two main kinds of travel. The first is the preliminary journey, when it is best to see as much as possible in a short time. The second is the planned travel, preceded by study. This was my preliminary tour of Viet-Nam, so I was prepared for anything. I sat down in a street-stall for a supper of curried beef and steamed frogs. A Viet-Namese sitting opposite sensed I was a newcomer and began to talk. He had studied biology in Paris and now gave lessons bringing in 10,000 piastres a month, i.e. about £100. He expounded his personal philosophy as if we were in a Hampstead pub. Such an encounter would be almost unheard of in Cambodia, where far fewer people have had a French education. I let him talk, intellectualizing everything as if he was a European. All westerners were scientists, he said. He wanted us to learn from Confucius the doctrine of the East that man is man and not material.

'I watch my students change,' he said. 'They begin to think. *Cogito ergo sum.* I find it thrilling to see this change taking place.'

My acquaintance was a violent anti-cleric. The Catholic religion, he announced, was mismanaged, misdirected, mis-every-thinged. Instead there should be a reformed, universal religion,

Communism if we liked, but the name would have to be changed. The Jews were trying to conquer the world, but Viet-Nam would not give in. Then he spoke freely about the shortcomings of the South Viet-Nam anti-Communist Government. The country's dollar-aided economy was in a hopeless state, he said, with coal and metals in pro-Communist North Viet-Nam, and rice in the anti-Communist South. 'It's going to change,' he said. I wondered if Government agents were listening in to this rather public conversation. 'During the War,' he continued, 'I helped British P.O.W.s escape from the Japanese. I never forget the English. I have friends – even' – he shook hands – 'in Newcastle.' I went to bed thinking how all these things mattered in Viet-Nam, and had to be discussed *ad nauseam*. In Cambodia they mattered hardly at all. This Viet-Namese teacher was speaking with the new voice of young Asia.

Although this was Viet-Nam, my hosts were Buddhist monks in Saigon's Cambodian monastery. They provide a roof for Cambodians on their way to what used to be called Cochin-China, where there is a considerable Cambodian minority. When I arrived at the monastery with a letter of introduction, my appearance was the same, *sans* beard, as that of a man whom I shall call Mr G.

Mr G's *décor* is a familiar sight on the main roads of Europe – a beard, rucksack, lean-and-hungry look. If you give him a lift in your car, you find he is aiming for Venice, and after Venice, Split, and after Split, who knows, and who cares anyway, since you are not going beyond Venice yourself. Mr G had strayed farther than his bearded comrades in Europe. Ceylon, Malaya, Siam, and finally Indo China. I met him when he was trying to hitch a boat-lift to Hong Kong. After that he had no particular plans. Japan, maybe, then home to the Midlands.

'You know,' he said, stifling a yawn. 'I've really seen too many countries, too many of their temples, too many museums.' True enough, he had seen too many, but too little of the ones he had seen. He had made, I remembered, a good impression on some English residents, who put him up for the night and saw him on to a boat to Hong Kong within two days. He did not have to pay and earned his passage looking after a herd of water-buffalo, only one of which died on the way. 'I'm not trying to go round the world,' he said. Anyway, he had in the course of his travels visited this Cambodian monastery in Saigon. Now, a few months after his visit, I was to see what sort of an impression this bearded traveller had made.

The Buddhist monks looked grimly at my rucksack. It seemed to remind them of something. After a long discussion I was invited to take off my shoes and go up to where the head monk was sitting. I remember his opening words.

'We had an Englishman here – a man with a beard. He stayed ten days.'

There was a pause.

'Ten days,' the monks repeated.

Then a layman spoke.

When we gave him rice, he wagged his head and ate it up. He didn't speak. One day he came back in the afternoon and expected a meal. You see, he didn't understand that Buddhist monks finish eating at midday.'

There was little, it seemed, that Mr G had understood. The Cambodians were most hospitable, but ten days had been too much for them. Mr G would have done better to stay in Ceylon, where his beard had earned him the job of extra in a film company's crowd scenes. A school contemporary of mine had recently accepted a challenge from the Duke of Edinburgh to go

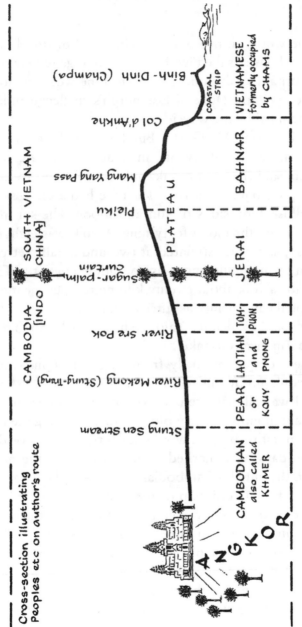

Fig. 1 – Cross-section illustrating peoples on author's route.

Cross-section illustrating Peoples etc on author's route

CAMBODIA [INDO   SOUTH VIETNAM   CHINA]

Angkor

CAMBODIAN also called KHMER   PEAR or KOUY   LAOTIAN and PNONG   TOM-PUON   JERAI   BAHNAR   VIETNAMESE formerly occupied by CHAMS

Stung Sen Stream   River Mekong (Stung-Trang)   River Sre Pok   Sugar-palm curtain   Pleiku   Mang Yang Pass   Col d'Ankhe   Binh-Dinh (Champa)   COASTAL STRIP

PLATEAU

round the world on five pounds. This kind of travel is all very well if he who wears the Five-Pound Look is genuinely representative of Britain's Adventurous Youth. One wonders how many people accepted the Duke of Edinburgh's challenge and whether any of them fell by the wayside.

After discussing Mr G, the Buddhist monks then asked my opinion on the latest events in space travel. According to Buddhism, said the head monk, nobody could go to the moon. They simply would not arrive. Then we had a discussion about the Buddhist dimensions of sun and moon. The sun measured fifty 'yoik', and the moon forty-nine. A yoik was eight hundred 'piam'. A 'piam' was estimated at two and a half metres, or the arm span from middle finger-tip to middle finger-tip. This reckoning made a yoik about twenty kilometres, but the monks said the accepted equivalent was fifteen kilometres.

'I give you these details,' said the head monk. 'So that you can warn the Americans to take care.'

The next day I was to fly from Saigon to Qui-Nhon. From there I would go by bus to Binh-Dinh and start on the road to Angkor. I was allowing ten weeks for the journey, and cut out the relevant months from an old calendar, marking the phases of the lunar months so that I would not forget the day or date. The full-moon days were marked with a circle, and the new-moon days with the initial – Cambodian initial – of the lunar month. I had also cut up an old map of Indo-China and pasted a section of it on to cardboard. I looked at the colours on the map – blue for the China Sea, a strip of red marking the coast of Viet-Nam, brown contours for the plateau, a broad blue strip for the River Mekong, then pale white, the Cambodian forest, all the way to Angkor. This, then, was the geographical pattern of my journey – coastal plain, plateau, River Mekong, Cambodian plain, Angkor in the forest. Everything was ready for the morrow except for colour films, which had failed to arrive. Later, I received a letter of apology from the film company saying that the order clerk had forgotten to carry out my order (*sic*).

CHAPTER THREE

FALSE START

It was not yet day. The chief monk rose from his bed and sounded a gong. It thundered round the silent monastery for a full two minutes. The monks woke, and at five a.m. assembled in the temple to recite Buddhist prayers. One of them wished me happiness on my journey – the traditional formula for a departing traveller. At the Saigon airport, a loudspeaker called out for Mr & Mrs L. I had met L once, an excellent young ethnologist, one of the few France has ever sent to Indo-China. His advice on the tribes at that moment would have been useful, but nobody appeared, so our plane took off without him. We were soon flying over forest-clad hills with the sea somewhere far away to our right. There were several stops, one at a hill-station where the air on the exposed runway was quite nippy. As we came into land at Qui-Nhon, capital of Binh-Dinh province, we caught a blazing glimpse of long sandy beaches, wooded islands and a blue sea. The town had been ransacked during the war and reconstruction was only just catching up. There were already one or two new buildings, the governor's anonymous-looking office and, of course, the missionary school with its Costa Brava view across the bay. The first hurdle was a discussion with the Governor's chief Secretary. It lasted one and a half hours, but since he was an extremely mild man the potentially contentious argument was kept on a friendly level.

He based his case for non-co-operation on the plea that there was insecurity in the regions I intended to visit. If the Viet-Minh

Communists abducted me, it might be awkward for me, but it would be even worse for the Government of South Viet-Nam, who would have to do some ticklish explaining. The Secretary also contended that my visa for travelling in South Viet-Nam was not valid. This argument was pure fantasy. I had entered Saigon at the airport, where passport, visa, and so on had all been checked. During the last twenty-four hours I had filled up three control forms for the Traffic Police. It seemed a bit late in the day to assert that I was not allowed to travel inside the country. I remembered my acquaintance who had friends 'even in Newcastle'. He had said among other things that the Government's control of South Viet-Nam went no farther than the city limits of the capital. There might be anarchy in the provinces. However, I had received assurances from the Government that perfect security reigned throughout the country. Foreigners were free to come and go as they liked.

The chief Secretary was not actually prepared to stop me going. After lunch of prawns fresh from the sea I decided to make a move from Qui-Nhon, the capital, to the village of Binh-Dinh about twenty miles farther north (see Map A). A bus was due to leave at three. It was really an old car, and its doors were held together with string. The driver-owner pulled away from the market-place punctually on the hour.

This was the country which had once been the ancient kingdom of Champa. On the right of our road there were two ancient Cham towers, one large and the other small. Out in front, we could see a third tower on a hill like Glastonbury Tor. At last we came to Binh-Dinh. From here a tricycle took me to the Copper Tower. This is the name given by the Viet-Namese to the only Cham monument which now remains within the ruins of Champa's northern capital. It is made of brick, not copper. This was the moment for which I had waited through long months of planning. We swerved down a cart-track, through a hamlet in the trees, up an incline to the foot of the Copper Tower standing proudly on its little hill. We were now on the coastal plain, facing the plateau, with our backs to the China Sea. As we approached the tower from the east, the sun was setting behind it. A track led away towards the hills. This was the route, I guessed, if not the actual road, which linked Champa to the ancient Khmer empire more than seven hundred years ago.

Before the last rays of the sun were gone, we descended from the tower and climbed up on to the ancient walls. Within the precinct of the city we could see ruins of a later Viet-Namese palace. The Viet-Minh Communists, themselves Viet-Namese, had destroyed it during the War. Its ruins were shabby beside the graceful brick tower, whose builders, the Chams, had long since been driven southwards by the Viet-Namese. There are no Chams living round Binh-Dinh today.

My Viet-Namese guide for the evening was the village photographer. He was also a dentist in his spare time. We spoke in French. He introduced me to the head of the village and an old man in charge of police affairs. They were courteous people and held a dinner for me at the village's expense. Eggs were plentiful the reverse of Cambodia where the Buddhist monks discourage poultry-breeding. In many Cambodian villages the peasants are so strict in their observance of Buddhist rules that anyone who tries to kill a chicken in public is immediately ostracized. Here, in Viet-Nam, there were no such restrictions.

After dinner the villagers asked if I would like to see 'Annamite theatre'. Since independence, the Viet-Namese no longer like being called 'Annamite' because it reminds them of their colonial past, but in common speech the two words seem almost

Journey's start: Binh-Dinh (Champa)

interchangeable. In this village I realized that the unsophisticated farmers did not mind being called 'Annamite'. It was the intellectuals I had met in the capital who preferred to be called 'Viet-Namese'.

The police-chief had a free season-ticket for the theatre show. He was also chief drummer, and beat out rhythm on his Annamite drum till late into the night. I was too tired to enjoy this rustic Viet-Namese drama, and in spite of the drum fell asleep several times during the performance. After the theatre ended, there was a conference with the head of the village. He suggested that my passport would be incomprehensible to people on the plateau. It would be wiser to have it translated into Viet-Namese before starting. This was a reasonable request, so I agreed to go back next morning to Qui-Nhon, the provincial capital.

There was a curfew in operation – nine o'clock except on nights when the theatre was playing. As for the Viet-Minh Communists, the old man was cryptic.

'They were here before,' he said. 'For many years. Now it's all finished, and yet ... they're still here. In the bushes, up the rafters, behind the chimney. Yes, the Viet-Minh are here all right. You know – they are the same race as ourselves.'

'Viet-Minh' is the best known of the many names given to those Viet-Namese who fought on the Communist side in the Indo-China war, and who today have their own Communist state – North Viet-Nam. The next morning the police-chief repeated his advice rather solemnly.

'I'm afraid,' he said, 'the villages on the plateau won't understand your passport. They may even think you're French. And they *hate* the French.'

So back I went to Qui-Nhon, the capital of the province, where a friend translated into Viet-Namese the words in my passport about Her Britannic Majesty. They are impressive in any language. I took the translation round to the chief Secretary for official certification. He was rather doubtful, and offered to telegraph his Government for special authority. I countered by offering to telegraph the British Embassy in a vague gesture of co-operation. Neither of us had much faith that the proposed telegrams would produce results, so much to the Secretary's relief I said I would go back to Saigon myself and sort the matter out. It was a disappointing decision after a long journey had brought me to the Copper Tower and the track leading westwards to

Angkor. Returning to Saigon with nothing begun was a bitter proposition.

There were other difficulties now. How could I go back and stay at the Cambodian monastery? The Buddhist monks would never understand why I had returned so quickly, and might doubt whether I had gone to Binh-Dinh at all. So instead I went to some Chinese friends in Cholon, the Chinatown of the Viet-Namese capital. Sunday night with Cambodians, Monday with Viet-Namese, and Tuesday with Chinese. How different these three Asian races were from each other – the way they washed, the way they talked, the way they spat. I did not mind them spitting, but did not actually pick up the habit myself. There were special spittoons in most of their eating and living-rooms.

One of the most ridiculous problems was 'dress'. My respectable clothes had been packed and sent by air to Pleiku, which was on the route from Champa to Angkor. If I was doomed to wage arguments with officials, it was essential to look reasonably tidy. My newest garment was a blue wind-jacket intended for cold weather on the plateau. I had no tie, so looked in the Chinese shops for a scarf. The tailors were making yellow-and-red flags for Independence Day, so I asked them to cut me a yellow square. Wrapped round the neck, it set off the blue of the jacket and, by chance, almost matched the yellow strap of my Japanese sandals. A Cambodian might disapprove of the Buddhist yellow being worn by me, but in Viet-Nam it looked nothing more than peculiar.

Tieless and sockless, I returned to the British Embassy, where people looked surprised to see me again so soon. The day was spent seeing officials at various Ministries. My bizarre clothing seemed to be having the opposite effect to what I had feared. I had not dared hope that within forty-eight hours I would be on

41

my way back to Qui-Nhon, bearer of a magic letter in French which outlined my itinerary. At the bottom it was stamped by the Ministry of the Interior. There was one disadvantage. I was not allowed to diverge from this straightforward itinerary, even if I found traces of my ancient Khmer road. Because of the bomb explosions in Saigon, I was warned that I must not let people think I was American. I had also been warned several times 'Don't let them think you're French'.

I decided to be English, which meant I had to equip myself with my country's flag before leaving Saigon, but there seemed to be no Union Jacks on sale. There were plenty adorning the Colombo Plan 1957 Conference buildings. I was planning to cut one of these down from its moorings when the British vice-consul produced two paper flags used for decorating car windscreens, Later, I managed to buy a Viet-Namese version of the British flag made of some light cloth. All its stripes were the same thickness. I gave the flag-dealer one of my paper flags so that his artisans could in future sew up a more correct version of the Union Jack. I felt that this action absolved me from planting the British flag on any ancient ruins which my journey might reveal.

I waited for the bus-taxi that would take me from Qui-Nhon back to Binh-Dinh. Only four days had passed since the first attempt. In the interval I had travelled a thousand kilometres by air, and was now ready to start. Once again I was in the taxi-bus, as it bumped its way north towards that ancient Cham tower, the Copper Tower. Now I noticed that the car had once belonged to a Monsieur R, whose home had been in Doubs, a French county in the foothills of the Alps. It was appropriate that on the eve of departure for Angkor there should be a reminder of Angkor's rediscoverer.

Henri Mouhot, who reached Angkor in 1860, was born at Montbéliard in the county of Doubs. An artist and photographer by inclination, he travelled all round Europe and had been in Russia teaching the families of the Grand-Dukes before the age of thirty. His brother married a relation of the African explorer, Mungo Park. If Mouhot had followed in Park's footsteps, he would have gone to Africa, but instead he went to the Far East and disclosed the ancient Khmer empire to an astonished world. Angkor had been known to missionaries down the centuries. Some of them, like the abbot who guided Mouhot, had actually seen the ruins. Mouhot's articles in the *Tour du Monde* fired the imagination of the French-speaking world with their tales of fabulous temples buried in the Cambodian jungle. As for Montbéliard, where Mouhot was born in 1826, it has a museum where Mouhot's botanical collections were once on view. Backed with British (not French) support, Mouhot embarked at Tilbury, London, and sailed for the East on 27th April, 1858. One hundred years later I found myself embarking on a journey which often brought reminders of Henri Mouhot's travels.

On the way to Binh-Dinh, we saw a man smoking a long pipe. He was standing in the market and seemed to be much taller than the average Viet-Namese. He was, I learnt, a tribesman who had come down from the plateau to sell his forest produce. He would return to his village with purchases of maize, salt and rice. The road was crowded with farmers wearing conical white straw hats. It was evening, and children flocked out from hutted schools. Houses were decorated with flags for the independence celebrations the next day. 'The ceremony is compulsory for everyone,' said the police-chief, but not apparently for an old man who volunteered to guide me round the wails of the ancient Cham capital. Early the next morning, the beaten mud-tracks were busy with peasants in collarless black blouses and black trousers. Many carried yellow flags with the three red stripes of

South Viet-Nam. Their old-fashioned-looking topees were coated with blue plastic cloth. This headgear is rarely worn nowadays by Europeans, but on Asian heads it still seems to give the wearer some sort of kudos. Many of the peasants rode in trim horse-traps. When the French arrived on this coastal strip in the late nineteenth century, wheeled vehicles were unknown. Yet, on the other side of the plateau, Cambodians had been using wheeled ox-carts ever since the days of the ancient Khmer empire.

The next day was spent pacing along the ramparts of the ancient Cham capital, the correct name for which is Cha-ban. It is sometimes referred to as Binh-Dinh, though the modern village of Binh-Dinh is not the one situated nearest the ruins. As we walked, the Copper Tower was seldom out of sight. I looked for traces of an ancient road leading west. Boots brought specially from England were uncomfortable in the heat, so I decided to try the local footwear – rubber sandals made from cast-off motor-car tyres. A suitable pair cost two shillings. They were not quite long enough, but I thought they would do. Once, when travelling in Greece, I sold spare motor-car tyres for this very purpose. Now I had a chance to try out the finished product. It seemed prudent to review the difficulties ahead. The first was whether my pass from the Ministry of the Interior would prove efficacious in the Interior. Second, would I find guides to take me through the tribal areas and bring me to Pim's village? Third, how when I finally reached Cambodia would the Cambodians react to a stranger emerging on foot from the Viet-Namese frontier?

For the moment, the real master of my destiny was the scrap of paper which I had achieved by my journey back to Saigon. In the afternoon I had to go and have it signed by the Rural District Commissioner, who was in the act of opening an Independence Day theatre show. His signature had to be stamped officially with a special stamp. An ex-private from the French Army led the way through the village to find this special stamp. It was a paradox that in independent Viet-Nam the old soldiers were immensely proud of their record in the French Army and talked about the Battle of the Somme if they could get the chance. We found the special stamp locked in a billiard saloon, where a pregnant woman was guardian of the key. She stamped the paper, increasing the number of special stamps to four. Later on the journey, extra leaves had to be pasted to the paper to make room for more and more special stamps. When we returned, the police-chief complained that the paper had been signed and stamped by the wrong person. There was also difficulty about guides, for my old retainer had renounced his duties, and there seemed for the moment nobody to replace him.

On this coastal plain in October the wet season was just beginning. Up on the plateau, where I would be soon, the rains were finishing, and I should have fine cool weather all the way to Angkor. The night was clear with the moon shining on its second day. This was the moon which waxed and waned as the journey went forward, and whose quarters I ticked off on a calendar specially prepared for this purpose. After sending a parcel of advance luggage to Pleiku by air, my rucksack weighed fifteen kilos, quite heavy enough for the tropical climate. I reviewed the medicine and clothes which made up this weight and decided nothing more could be jettisoned. As for budget – I reckoned to spend about ten shillings a day divided up as follows: five shillings for guides, two shillings for food, and three shillings for extras or emergencies. This estimate proved about right, though the living was not exactly regal. I carried one book – the first volume of Dante's *Divine Comedy*.

CHAPTER FOUR

UP TO THE PLATEAU

There were several tracks leading west from the ancient Cham capital, none of which gave evidence that it had once been an ancient Khmer road. The advantage of travelling on foot was that I could ask the local inhabitants about the road at regular intervals. The answers were almost always negative so it would be tedious to repeat them here and at every village along the way. As long as I was in Viet-Nam, I virtually restricted myself to having a look at the terrain through which the road would have to pass. I was not allowed to diverge from an itinerary which ran almost due east–west. Under these circumstances, my first objective on leaving Binh-Dinh was Pim's village, which as I explained earlier had nothing to do with the Khmer road, but which promised certain *divertissement* if I could find it.

After much bargaining and saving of face, my previous day's guide, the old man, agreed to come with me on this first morning of the journey to Angkor. Setting off west from the Copper Tower, we soon left the walls of the ancient Cham capital behind us. We waded across a stream and then found a path leading to a village. From here it was a good twenty-kilometre walk, first through laterite quarries and over moorland, then weaving among the on-stretching ricefields. The sun was already hot when we started, for arguments with the guide had lost precious hours of cool walking-time. Indo-China is in the northern hemisphere, which means that October is a winter month, but the days are only a little shorter than in summer. In a country where the hot temperature hardly changed it seemed incongruous to have longer and shorter days. The Viet-Namese peasants stared at us sullenly. I might have been mistaken, but into this sullen stare from peasants I read all the unforgotten hatred of the Indo-China war.

Towards midday the sun became unbearably hot. The old man said he was hungry, so we stopped in a village. Our meal was served in what seemed at first to be a small Viet-Namese temple. It was really a private house with a family altar flanked on each side by a bed. There was a single phrase writ large on the wall, which I looked up in my pocket dictionary and found meant 'joyful'. I smiled at the old guide, and pointed the word out to him. He tried to read it, but the percentage of illiteracy was high among old men prepared to guide Englishmen across ricefields under a raging sun. He had received a traditional family education, and could read Chinese characters, which the Viet-Namese used for writing till a Portuguese missionary invented a romanized alphabet which could cope with the extra tones, sounds, and consonants which we lack.

About three in the afternoon we continued our journey. Foothills flanking the pass up to the plateau loomed larger and began to close in from north and south. We passed three more ancient Cham towers, stately like those I had already seen on the road to Binh-Dinh. The Government claimed to be keeping them clear of weeds, while local people said that they had been partly demolished by the Viet-Minh Communists. By evening we had come to a broad, shallow river, on the other side of which lay a market town. Water sparkled as the ferryman punted his bamboo sailing-boat to meet us. Before the War this town had a silk-factory. It was destroyed during the fighting, and had not yet been rebuilt. The chief of police was young and forthcoming.

'The Viet-Minh are living on the plateau,' he said, 'among the tribes. We have ten here. Sometimes they come down to the villages and give instructions to wives whose husbands are in North Viet-Nam. Tracts and Communist newspapers are distributed. Keep faith in Ho Chi Minh, they tell our people. Nothing to worry about.' He then made a remark which I was used to hearing – 'the people in this town hate the French'. He gave several reasons for this hatred. The Viet-Minh Communists had occupied the area for a long time. Ten years of Communist propaganda had left its mark. Another reason, so he said, was the people's memory of the French colonialists. As for the possibility of a reunited Viet-Nam, he was adamant. It was not the first time in Viet-Namese history that the country had been divided against itself.

I slept in the military post. While I lay dozing, Viet-Namese soldiers chanted Roman Catholic prayers, not in Latin but in their own language. For though the Christian missionaries were unsuccessful in Cambodia, they made many converts in Viet-Nam. The type of Buddhism practised in Viet-Nam previously was Mahayana, the Northern School. It is still observed by some Viet-Namese, but has none of the force of Southern School Buddhism, which flourishes in Cambodia. The Cambodians have tolerated missionaries for centuries, letting them build churches and even a cathedral, but they are as Buddhist now as they ever were in the days of Angkor. Though there is little effort by the Buddhists of Cambodia to proselytize, a number of Viet-Namese have recently adopted Southern School Buddhism, and have their own monastery in Saigon. Viet-Namese prayers, whether Christian or Buddhist, remind the listener, as they reminded me in this military outpost, of nothing more holy than a pack of wolves baying at the moon.

A new guide was provided the next morning. Just before leaving, I was summoned by the chief of police.

'Three of you will go up the pass,' he said, 'not two.'

A young man in black sidled up behind him. What was the reason for this extra guide?

'Do I pay him?' I asked the Chief.

'No,' was the reply. 'He'll just travel with you. That's all.'

After a few hundred yards, I looked over my shoulder to see if the third man was following. There was no sign. I never knew where he went, or why I was told he would come with us. Was he skirting through the bushes or what? According to my itinerary, we were not allowed to diverge from the road number nineteen till reaching the presumed site of Pim's village. The new guide was a young man who set such a spanking pace that I had difficulty in keeping up. I began to regret the old fellow of the previous day who had hurried back to Binh-Dinh, much pleased with his pay. It was no joke walking on the farmer road nineteen. The metalled surface had disintegrated, and it was half remade with unrolled chunks of rock. Stones cut into the soles of the feet. Because of flooding in the south, this old French road was being used by heavy traffic. There were no private cars, only military and commercial trucks, which thundered past, leaving the road in a worse state than it was before. Houses thinned out, and the road rose more steeply. 'No Refreshments Available' was how the latest guidebook kept travellers away from this part of Viet-Nam. When the sun became too hot, we stopped at a wattle hut. A small girl served hard-boiled eggs wrapped in chupatty dipped in fish juice. There were fresh mint leaves and onion stalks. The guide drank two pints of tea. I drank four. It looked like water from a Cotswold pond, but was infinitely refreshing.

After one and a half days of the car-tyre sandals, my feet were shaping better than I expected. I washed off the dust and discovered five nascent blisters, which I then swathed in sticking-plaster. Meanwhile, the guide took out a dirty piece of paper from his shirt pocket and began writing earnestly. The road became like the purlieus of a quarry. When night fell, we had covered twenty-eight kilometres, and had spent nearly half our time in climbing the *Col d'Ankhé*. When we reached the top there was a magnificent view looking back, like a northward glance from the top of Roncesvalles in the Pyrenees. The river we had crossed the previous evening was still visible. Hidden beyond lay what had once been the ancient kingdom of Champa.

An army truck had just come off the road near a bridge at the summit and crashed thirty feet down into the bushes. The windscreen was smashed. By a stone, or a bullet? I told the soldiers I was expecting Viet-Minh Communists to arrive any moment. They laughed and said there were no saboteurs within three or four days' walking distance of the col. The village, when at last we reached it, looked dark and miserable. A young man led the way to a mountain stream where I bathed. When we returned, a royal supper was served, including an omelette made from six duck eggs, which I finished single-mouthed. A young girl watched us. She was the policeman's wife. I had never seen a Viet-Namese girl wear a Norwegian sweater, and the red reindeer galloped incongruously across her delicate Asian breasts.

Two hours' walk in the morning brought us to Ankhé, once an important centre, but today only the skeleton of a town. There was no post office, and many of the shops were shut up or abandoned. It was exciting to see that we had well and truly left the coastal plain. Ankhé marked the beginning of tribal country, the Plateau, or P.M.S., as it is called, *Pays des Montagnards du Sud.*

Tribesmen with long hair were strolling in the streets, wearing loin-cloths, and baskets strapped to their backs. This was the beginning of Pim's country. His tribe, the Bahnars, cultivate rice in several ways. Some moved through the forest, cutting ricefields on the side of hills, which they soon abandoned, going on to make new ones. Others had permanent ricefields, beside which they established villages. Where should I look for Pim's people and Pim's village?

We tramped to the Government offices, shabby and unsign-posted. A small man with a toothbrush moustache was standing in the forecourt. His clothes were half a soldier's and half civilian, and included a khaki tunic on which there was a row of medals, the *Légion d'Honneur* among others. As the small man turned to meet us, his face reminded me of Charlie Chaplin. He walked inquisitively across the courtyard. Just then a Viet-Namese soldier emerged from the office and asked to see my famous paper from the Ministry of the Interior. He read the itin-erary out loud, starting from the beginning. When he came to the piece about Pim's village he read it slowly and a smile spread across his face.

'This man knows the village,' he said, pointing at the little man with the moustache. 'He's a *montagnard* himself.'

I turned to the little man and said excitedly, 'Do you know of the famous Bahnar chieftain, Pim, who died hereabouts in 1934?'

'I'm the son of his brother,' replied the little man. It was a recognition scene worthy of a Greek play. He brought me up to date on recent history of Pim's village. It turned out that I was speaking to a living member of Pim's family. To make sure I asked another question. 'Who was Pim's father?' 'Bok Pim's father was Bok Kiem,' he replied. 'I am the son of Bok Mohr, the brother of Bok Pim. My name is Siu-Rhing.' 'Bok' was the Bahnar prefix of respect for a man. Other tribesmen gathered round. They heard the names of these three Bahnar Caesars ring out across the courtyard – Bok Kiem, Bok Pim, Bok Mohr. Siu-Rhing said next that Pim's days were the good old days and that now the Bahnar tribe could boast no chieftains like Mohr, Pim, and Kiem. Bok Kiem had been the greatest soldier. His son, Bok Pim, had won fame not only as a negotiator but also as a fighter. Bok Mohr, who survived Pim by twenty years, was an administrator, and at the end of his life patriot and warrior. Before talking more about Pim, Siu-Rhing was anxious to tell me about his own father, Mohr. 'When Bok Pim died in 1934,' he said, 'Bok Mohr became the most famous chieftain in the region. Actually he had reigned jointly with Bok Pim since 1912.'

In the Government's office there was a large-scale map. I had studied a similar one at the Institute of Historical Research. It marked two villages of Plei Bon. I now guessed why. 'Yes,' said Siu-Rhing. 'The village in the west belonged to my father, Bok Mohr. Bok Pim's village lies on the east of the stream. Among our people these villages are known as Plei Bon Mohr and Plei Bon Pint. You will see. Don't worry – I will send the news to my village and call the relatives of Bok Pim to meet you.'

Then he told the story of how Mohr had defended the village against the Viet-Minh Communists, and was eventually captured. Already an old man, he died in prison after several months' captivity. People said he was poisoned by the Viet-Minh. Mohr's death marked the end of Bahnar resistance. Siu-Rhing had been evacuated with the retreating French Army. He lived to fight again, so fiercely that the Viet-Minh Communists put a price on his head. They did not want the eldest son of Mohr to rally the Bahnar cause. Meanwhile, Siu-Rhing lost contact with his fellow-villagers. They deserted the ashes of Plei Bon Mohr for a time and fled into the hills. There many of them remained living on roots and leaves till the end of hostilities. I had many things to discuss with Siu-Rhing, but we could not move from Ankhé till the Governor's delegate arrived. I spent most of the day resting. Good luck had helped me on my way to Pim's village. The delegate arrived in the evening. He was a young army lieutenant, pleasant and very practical.

'I've just been out on patrol,' he said. 'We make two operations a month. This time we found a cache of twelve Communist rifles. I think there must be hundreds more dotted round the mountains, but how can one hope to find them all?'

He arranged for a tribesman to go with me the next day as armed escort. There were said to be tigers on the road. I was taken aback to find that our speed was scaled to the walking powers of a Bahnar tribesman. We might be expected to do fifty kilometres at a stretch. The departure was planned for just before dawn. I went to bed early, regretting that I had sent my sleeping-bag by air to Pleiku. The nights on the plateau were much colder than along the coastal plain. By four a.m. it was bitter. Before waking I dreamt the following dream. I was reading the lesson in church, a piece from the Old Testament. The text ran something like this. 'Bok Kiem lived many years and he died. And after Bok Kiem, his son Bok Pim lived many years and died. And Pim had houses.' Then, as often happens when I dream about reading the lesson in church, I lost the place and went on repeating the words 'And Pim had houses ... and Pim had houses'. That was all, except the puzzled look on the faces of the congregation, especially the older folk, who were trying to remember if the story of Pim came from Deuteronomy or the Apocrypha.

CHAPTER FIVE

DRINKS ON THE HARVEST

This was what I liked – an early start with twelve kilometres walked before half-past eight. We saw no tigers, only a place on the road where they said a tiger had eaten someone down to his waist. Soon after dawn two Bahnar tribesmen met us on the road. Siu-Rhing had asked them to help us on our way to Plei Bon. I had stocked up with presents before leaving town – a thousand cigarettes for the adults and two kilograms of bonbons for the children. We stopped once or twice for a rest, and I caught cold after bathing in a mountain stream. Rice was taken at a wooden hut, where the guides drank pints and pints of tea, while they talked to some Viet-Namese who bought their tobacco in exchange for rice.

In the afternoon another pass, called Mang Yang (Gate of the Gods), rose up in front, as steep but not as long as the *Col d'Ankhé*. It was a stiff climb all the same. Before we reached the top, our way was barred by a green snake four and a half feet long. The tribesmen ran back down the hill and began throwing stones. In fury, the snake turned viciously and darted down the track towards us. I could see its head raised two or three inches from the ground. The tongue darted in and out. Soon it gave up the chase and disappeared into the long grass. I asked my companions what kind of snake this was. When translated, the words just meant 'green snake'.

One or two Viet-Namese were living in huts on the crest of the pass. The food was first-class. My Bahnar tribesmen, in their loin-cloths, were not accustomed to sitting down in a bistro, but they attacked the food like starving mariners. We ate in silence for an hour. I shared a bottle of beer with the armed escort, whose name was Beunon. The others sipped pure alcohol, at a fraction the price of our beer. One of the soldiers signed my piece of paper from the Ministry of the Interior. He may have been a Bahnar serving in the Viet-Namese army, because he had difficulty in writing and did not know where to put the accents on. Some of the soldiers, he explained, were tribesmen. With hair cut short, and trousers instead of loin-cloths, they looked not unlike Cambodians. Their speech-tunes seemed the same also and there were word similarities. The first one I noticed was *m'chnam*, which meant 'one year' in Bahnar and Cambodian. These Bahnar soldiers in the Viet-Namese Army earned four hundred piastres (about £4) a month. The corporals earned double. Viet-Namese soldiers of the same rank in the same army earned rather more.

We were slow moving away from the pass in the morning. Thirty-three kilometres on the previous day had left the party weary. After another cold night we felt chilled to the bone. The road number nineteen did not go through Bahnar villages, since most of them lay off the road, a few kilometres north or south. After several hours' walk we stopped beside two big trees on the right of the road. This, my guides told me, was the site of Pim's cousin's grave. The trees had been planted at the time of his death. Today, looking between them, we could see the rooftops of a Bahnar village on the opposite hillside. This was one of the villages inhabited at different times by Kiem and Pim when they were on the move in time of tribal war.

About half-past nine we left the road number nineteen and took to a jungle path, first through a bamboo wood, then light forest. A tiger had been killed here two days before. We saw some deer. It was good to get away from the stony surface underfoot. The path grew narrower, and Beuon stopped for a moment to load his rifle, then continued, peering into the undergrowth as he went.

Beuon explained why he was so cheerful. He had several wives, one of whom lived in Plei Bon Mohr. Guiding me was like having a forty-eight-hour pass to visit his family. He spoke fluent French, so none of my questions went unanswered. Another two hours' walk brought us out of the forest into a patch of ripe paddy. A Viet-Namese village lay across the path, and we sat down in the police-station for the usual formalities. Then fifteen minutes' walk up the track led to a gap in the bushes. Pim's village, quite separate from the Viet-Namese village we had just left, was visible on the hillside, little more than one kilometre distant. I asked Beuon about the house I could see with, a high thatch.

Not Pim's house,' he said. 'That is the *maison commune* where bachelors sleep. Women are not allowed.'

Emerging from the forest, we crossed the deserted site where Mohr's village had been burnt to the ground. It had been rebuilt a few hundred yards farther on. Very trim, there stood the village of Plei Bon Mohr, nearly a hundred houses strong. It was evidently more important than Plei Bon Pim on the other side of the valley. Siu-Rhing, Pim's nephew, had been granted special leave to come and join us, but would not be arriving till the next day. We waited under a tree for the headman's permission to enter the village. Then we made our way to the *maison commune*, a beautiful log but on stilts with a swerving thatched roof, high, like the roof I had seen across the valley in Pim's village. Inside the *maison commune* of Mohr's village there were four wooden columns attached to the floor – totem poles, I call them, for want of a more correct term. The villagers said they had been put there by the orders of Bok Kiem and Bok Pim. I noted that both these gentlemen had been long dead when the *maison commune of* Plei Bon Mohr was rebuilt. The tribesmen have very little sense of history.

Beuon ran off and returned leading a procession of a dozen venerable-looking Bahnars. 'These are the gentry,' he said. I bowed to each one respectfully. They bowed in return. We shook hands solemnly. Some of them clasped right-hand wrist with left hand as an added sign of respect. This showed they accepted completely the polite action of shaking hands, a custom which was not new to the Bahnars, but had long been established as a form of tribal greeting, so they said. The notables of the village crouched round in a circle. I offered cigarettes and distributed sweets to a knot of inquisitive children. Beuon made a speech, and read out the letter of introduction which Siu-Rhing had sent along in advance. I added a few words saying how pleased I was to meet the descendants of Bok Pim and Bok Mohr. At this moment a tubercular-looking old man came tottering up the narrow wooden steps. The raised doorway of a Bahnar building can be reached only by walking up the kind of thing used in England for hens to enter henhouses. The Bahnar 'hen-runs' were often rather narrow. I feared this particular hen-ramp would tip over every time someone came up it.

The old man was the local Bahnar chieftain, as opposed to the administrative headman appointed by the Government. This chieftain was an old man venerated by all the Bahnars in the neighbourhood, with certain exceptions, as I discovered later. He was introduced as the young, maybe youngest, brother of the deceased chieftain, Pim. His name was similar, and he was known as 'Bok Phinh'. Bok Phinh's first words were a solemn invitation to take part in the Feast of the First Harvesting of Rice. This, the last day of October, was a *jour de fête,* during which the tribesmen stayed away from the ricefields. They would spend the time revelling on alcohol brewed from few-days-old ripe paddy. A pig had been killed as sacrifice for the festival. Its interesting remains had been cooked, and were now lying wrapped in leaves beside one of the drinking-jars. I asked about Pim's jars, the ones he had been so fond of and shown proudly to the French explorers in the nineteenth century. All had perished, they said, but the next day I was shown an old earthenware jar reputed to have belonged to Bok Pim. It was a big jar and came up to my thigh when I stood beside it.

We were sitting in a space near Phinh's house, which was thoroughly exposed to the sun. Each man had to drink five measures on the day of the feast. Rice, including the husks, had been standing in jars for more than a week. Today water had been added. As it seeped down the jar, a most potent drink was created. The Bahnars drank from the base of the jar with hollow slivers of bamboo acting as straws. They were, rather like hollow flexible curtain-rods.

The measure was determined by a dipstick which hung from a fulcrum athwart the jar's mouth. Before the drinker started drinking through his bamboo 'straw', water would be poured into the jar till it began to overflow. This was the moment to start sipping. As the alcohol disappeared up the 'straw' into the drinker's mouth, liquid would stop overflowing and begin to sink below the jar's lip. When the liquid sank below the end of the dipstick and allowed it to swing freely without touching the surface, a measure was deemed to have been drunk. More water was then added till the jar overflowed again. Then it was someone else's turn.

The dipstick was a slip of bamboo about half an inch long. The jar's diameter was so wide that drinking half an inch of liquid was a hefty draught. I recalled in a flash the combined experiences of previous travellers in this region. But as 'the English Bok Pym', there was no escape. I had to drink the maximum of toasts. Already tired after our thirty-six-hour journey from Ankhé we were now exposed to a pitiless sun, which Phinh and fellow patriarchs did not seem to notice.

For the next two days, Beuon and I went in and out of an alcoholic stupor. Drinks were on the harvest. Every time I settled in the *maison commune*, an invitation would come from the village to 'have a jar'. We drank, that was the main recollection. Beuon became red in the face, and admitted that he often went tipsy on the stuff, even though he was used to it. He also said that he had another wife in a village down the road. She was better-looking than the wife here at Plei Bon, he said. At this first session, Bok Phinh watched me drink from the first and fifth jars. Then we drank together from a spare jar in honour of my arrival. After these odd aperitifs I looked drunkenly at Beuon, who came to the rescue. There existed an old tribal custom whereby I could invite all the company to drink the same number of measures as myself. In this drinking joust the company boiled down to Phinh, who for all his tuberculosis drank more than all of us and never turned a hair. While Phinh drank, I asked the others about Pim. I put no faith in the accuracy of their answers. They recounted the living tradition, no more and no less.

Pim, it seemed, was not a big man, but when he mounted an elephant, the elephant fell down. If he mounted a horse the horse fell down. Once the French made him a present of a mule. When he mounted the mule it fell down. Pim had been a rich man, and his house was a hundred metres long, full of gongs and jars.

All the tribes from miles around came to Pim's house and paid homage. One day the house was struck by lightning and everything was burnt. Thus ended the riches of Bok Pim, but his fame as a chieftain continued till death. Was Pim a warrior, first and foremost, or a man of peace? This was the question. 'A man of peace,' replied the tribesmen. 'But if necessary, he made war to obtain peace.' This, then, was Pim, a chieftain known to every Bahnar in the region. Yes, my two travelling companions had heard of him, though they came from distant villages. They also knew about Mohr, but Kiem was too far back for their memories.

Sun roasted our uncovered heads. The rice wine settled on an empty stomach. I rose from jar number five with difficulty, when Phinh proposed lunch. Beuon was unsteady on his legs. We staggered towards Phinh's house, and sank thankfully into the shadows. Late in the afternoon some food was set before us – rice and sacrificial pork. My recollections after this meal were hazy. I remembered hearing someone expound a family tree, from which it seemed that Phinh was Pim's first cousin. Then I sat on and broke a pair of sunglasses. While we grovelled round looking for the bits, someone else said that Christian Mass had been abolished in this district. At any rate, the *curé* was hardly ever seen. If I wanted to go to church I would have to wait until I reached Kontum, a biggish town – not on my route, or the Ministry of the Interior's itinerary. Throughout my visit to Plei Bon I never fathomed just who they thought I was, and whether they realized how absurd was the connection, or rather lack of connection, between 'Pym' and 'Pim'. I dare say it will serve me right if one day some tribesman yet unborn knocks at the front door in his loin-cloth and says he's one of the family.

CHAPTER SIX

PIM'S PUNISHMENT

The next day I visited the tribal school and witnessed the ceremony of Bahnar children saluting the Viet-Namese colours. Fifty
minute children in ragged loin-cloths lined up round the flag and
sang marching songs in honour of the Viet-Namese President,
Ngo Dinh Diem. 'I have to teach Annamite,' said the Bahnar
schoolmaster, 'even though I don't really know any myself.'
He talked to me in goodish French. In the evening the children
gathered in the *maison commune* and sang special songs in my
honour – Bahnar songs, I hoped, when I heard what they were
planning, but they sang with gusto the ever-recurring words
'Hurrah for President Ngo Dinh Diem'.

According to Siu-Rhing, the Viet-Namese were not allowed to
build houses inside the Bahnar communities. As for the village
we had passed on our way up, it was said that the population
had collaborated with the Viet-Minh Communists during the
occupation. Many of them had been sent to prison by Siu-Rhing
himself when the area was liberated. 'So they know me well,'
Siu-Rhing informed me with a smile. 'Even though I am not
Viet-Namese.' Though he was a Bahnar tribesman and not Viet-
Namese, Siu-Rhing worked for the Viet-Namese Government,
and was a paid civil servant. Fifteen kilometres from Plei Bon
there was a new Viet-Namese village populated by refugees.
How, I wondered, were the genial Bahnars reacting to this
invasion which was bringing Viet-Namese settlements to every
corner of the plateau? I asked them how they felt. 'We are under

orders,' they replied calmly. 'We are the *montagnards*. We have our ricefields, but we have no guns and no aeroplanes. Before, we were under orders of the French. Now we must obey the Viet-Namese. Some of us had guns for hunting. Now they have been impounded. The police gave us a receipt, but what use is a piece of paper for killing tigers or deer?' I often heard this complaint.

An important visitor was announced. It turned out to be Bok Bieng, who was headman, and acknowledged chieftain, of Plei Bon Pim. There were formal introductions, and short speeches, after which Bieng presented me with a hen for supper. Would I care to visit Plei Bon Pim? This was the moment for which I had waited since we caught our first glimpse of Pim's village the previous day. Down we went across the ricefields, over a stream, and up a sharp rise to the *maison commune*. Pim's village was slightly nearer the stream than Mohr's. Bieng was the nearest descendant of Pim I had yet encountered. According to living memory, which I would say was most unreliable, Bieng was the grandson of Pim. Here is the family tree as expounded by Bok Bieng.

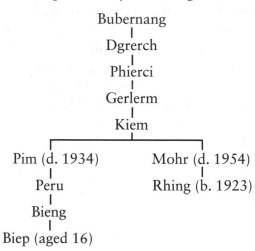

Bubernang
|
Dgrerch
|
Phierci
|
Gerlerm
|
Kiem

Pim (d. 1934)   Mohr (d. 1954)
| |
Peru   Rhing (b. 1923)
|
Bieng
|
Biep (aged 16)

Arriving at Pim's village

The recent history of Pim's village was mysterious. Why, for instance, was Plei Bon Mohr destroyed by the French and not Plei Bon Pim? Even after long conversations with Siu-Rhing I could not be certain what really happened. My first impression was that Mohr's village had been destroyed by the Viet-Minh Communists. After probing, I discovered it had been bombed by the French. There could be two possible reasons for this. Either the French had information that the village was harbouring rebels, or the Viet-Minh Communists pretended to occupy the village and then withdrew, leaving tell-tale signs which the French mistakenly bombed. The Viet-Minh Communists had good reason for wanting the village destroyed. Mohr had been

63

a friend of the French for a long time. It was all cunningly done, for afterwards they could say that the French wantonly destroyed Plei Bon Mohr with their bombs.

According to Siu-Rhing, when the Viet-Minh Communists occupied the area they destroyed the houses and property belonging to the families of Pim and Mohr. When the Bahnars surrendered, those who remained in Mohr's village were governed in two groups, pro- and anti-Communist. By two groups I thought he meant Plei Bon Mohr and Plei Bon Pim. Wrong again. Less important than Plei Bon Mohr, Plei Bon Pim had not been destroyed by anyone. It began to look as if Bieng must have been a collaborator. When I asked Siu-Rhing about this, he replied darkly: 'The words of Bok Bieng are good, but his heart is bad. Loyalty is the first duty of a good *montagnard*.'

Anyway, I found Bieng very congenial. He was younger than Phinh, and his brain functioned more quickly. We sat among the jars in his long wooden house and drank the customary measures – two for him, two for his assistants, and two for his wife. The wheels thus oiled, Bieng agreed to lead us to the burial-ground of his grandfather, Pim. The other tribesmen, who had not been drinking, were less keen. The way to the burial-ground was overgrown with jungle. A tiger had been seen that very morning stealing goats on the far side of the village. Bieng led the way out of the village on a track leading east. After thirty minutes he turned off into the bush, hacking a path through the thick grass and shrubs. Very soon we came to the remains of a deserted Bahnar cemetery.

The dead were buried inside wooden palisades, the stakes of which were sculptured on the top like the inverted domes of large solid bells. Sometimes they were carved in the shape of a man. The dead man's jars were placed over his body. Sometimes

Plei Bon: the wife of Bok Bieng

Plei Bon: the family of Bok Pim

Sometimes they were carved in the shape of a man

we stumbled on the tops of these jars where the wooden palisade had rotted and disappeared. The forest was reclaiming its lost land. This, said Bieng, was the former site of Pim's village. It was here that he established his famous long house, longer than any existing today in either village. Here, his jars, and here, his gongs. At the far end of the burial-ground there were remains of an impressive palisade – the one we were looking for. The sky was overcast. In the darkness of the wood the stakes took on a human look, sentinels of their former master, the warrior Pim.

'And where,' I asked, 'is the spirit of Bok Pim?'

'The spirit of Bok Pim,' they said, 'has passed into the members of Bok Pim's family.'

They never seemed to use a possessive adjective, always repeating the name, 'Bok Pim' this, 'Bok Pim' that. The Bahnars had no god, only a multitude of genies and spirits, the most powerful of which lived where we stood reverently – in the forest. Bieng threw a pinch of tobacco towards Pim's grave and said something under his breath. Beuon translated the prayer: 'We come only to see. Please forgive us and allow us to return to our houses without catching any disease.' Near Pim's grave the forest was overgrown. We cleared a path up to the decaying palisade. All was quiet except for the cry of a jungle-bird. Beyond Pim's grave was the grave of his wife. She died before him, when Bieng was still a small boy. Yellow daisies were growing in the bushes. I picked one of these daisies and with the tribesmen's approval tossed it over the palisade.

Then I was told why Pim's house had been struck by lightning. Tradition said that in his old age Bok Pim began imitating Viet-Namese customs. This was the reason which the Bahnars offered for the fact that his house had been destroyed by fire from heaven. I asked why was it such a great crime to 'imitate Viet-Namese customs'. What shocked the tribesmen most was that Pim began bowing to sacred objects like Buddhas. He began going down on his hands and knees, clasping his hands in a reverential un-tribal way. This was the reason offered, apocryphal surely, for Pim's punishment, and it took me to the heart of the question which I had uppermost in my mind – 'Now that the French have left Indo-China for good, will these tribes ask for independence?' Independence from whom, or what? From their new masters, of course, the Viet-Namese, whom they have always disliked, so much so that now they tell this fable about how their most famous chieftain's house was struck by lightning for no more serious offence than adopting Viet-Namese customs and dress. In other words, they seem to have fabricated this story of Pim's punishment to fit their new circumstances. Once upon a time they roamed freely over the plateau, fighting other tribes. The French brought peace, then the French went and more colonizers moved in – the Viet-Namese. The tribesmen had no means of resisting this Viet-Namese penetration. As they kept on saying pathetically, '*Nous n'avons plus de fusils.*' The whole business reminded me untidily of the ancient Greek general, Pausanias, who towards the end of his life went about in a Median dress and kept a Persian table, both of which habits should have been anathema to a Greek. For the Greeks, substitute the Bahnars, Pim for Pausanias and the Viet-Namese for Medes and Persians. The comparison is not, as I say, very tidy, but did Pim really go about in a Viet-Namese dress and keep a Viet-Namese table? Or were the Bahnars making the whole thing up? I suppose there is little evidence that Pim wore any dress at all, except a loin-cloth which is how his descendants clothe themselves, or I should say do not clothe themselves, today. It was all most odd, and I was determined to extract every ounce of meaning from this strange story. Was there a moral here for Siu-Rhing, who had himself adopted Viet-Namese customs in a big way? He worked as liaison officer between the tribes and the Viet-Namese Government. He was in charge of Ankhé district, in which, I learnt with surprise, the Bahnar population was estimated at 25,000. Siu-Rhing was too young to be a chieftain – he was in his thirties. Yet, as the eldest son of Mohr, and a soldier in his own right, he would remain an important leader for the rest of his life. When I heard that his own eldest son had died suddenly a few weeks earlier, I wondered whether a repetition of Pim's punishment was not about to be re-enacted. The complicated relationships in these tribal villages were beginning to unfold themselves in a fascinating sequence. The next morning I found myself suddenly involved.

Before returning to Plei Bon Mohr, for further drinking-bouts, I had some more drinks with Bieng. As a bachelor, I avoided having to drink two measures on behalf of my wife. Bieng's measure was almost an inch long. The fulcrum, made of polished wood, looked like a boomerang. In Plei Bon Mohr they used old pieces of bamboo which would be thrown away at the end of the session. Bieng's house was full of jars. Sure enough one of them had belonged to Bok Pim. Had it survived the fire, or come from another of Pim's villages? Nobody knew. I wanted to move it into the sunlight and take a photograph. Bieng said it must not be moved from its place by the wall 'except for drinking'.

A Bahnar chieftain's wealth was measured by his jars. An old jar, worth twenty slaves in the time of Pim, was now said to be worth five, ten, and sometimes fifteen oxen. Viet-Namese merchants made imitations of the designs and handles, which they would reproduce on new jars, trying to pass them off as antiques. The tribesmen boasted that they were themselves great jar connoisseurs and could easily detect a jar which was not genuinely old. Siu-Rhing had been selling off his jars – a pity, I felt, but he made no bones about being a modernist. He, too, claimed to own one of Pim's jars, which had come down to him as an heirloom from Pim's brother, Mohr. He said it was worth thirty oxen, and claimed Bieng's was only worth twenty. He justified his own jar-selling by a tradition – I began to wonder how old some of these traditions were – that if you possessed more than two old jars fire would descend on the house. Old jars were said to carry evil spirits. The evil spirit of a solitary jar was said to be stronger than all others. Since Siu-Rhing and Bok Bieng both owned solitary jars, former property of Bok Pim, I deduced that they were both equally plagued by evil spirits, which would account for a good deal.

Although Siu-Rhing was working for an anti-Communist government, he did not hate the Viet-Minh Communists for political reasons. He hated them for killing his father, the chieftain Mohr. Whether they did in fact kill Mohr was not relevant. Rhing believed this murder took place. The real force in his life was tribal vengeance – vengeance for his father's death. Foulest of modern wars, the war in Indo-China would not soon be forgotten. One day it would recede into the past, then, like the events in the life of chieftain Pim, the tribesmen would forget what really had happened. Siu-Rhing was faced with the same dilemma which faces all these tribesmen. Where does their duty lie? As paid lackeys of their Viet-Namese rulers, or as champions of their own peoples fighting for independence from the depths of the forests and the tops of the mountains? I remembered that these were the tribesmen whom King Marie, the Frenchman, had once described as 'independent'. After my visit to Pim's village I took an enthusiastic interest in the process of 'Viet-Namization' which the Viet-Namese Government was pursuing in these tribal areas. Later I was able to compare its success to some extent with the process of 'Cambodianization' taking place within similar tribal areas on the other side of the Viet-Namese–Cambodian frontier.

Meanwhile, the tribesmen plied me with drink. After eight measures I tried to sum up my impressions. Plei Bon – both halves – was one of the tidiest villages I had ever seen. Firewood was piled neatly under the houses. The courtyards were swept clean. The dogs were healthy, and pigs plentiful. On the slope near the ricefields there were several dozen little wooden granaries, which were not locked. The Bahnars of Plei Bon were proud of the fact that no thieves lived among their number. If a thief was detected, the villagers would condemn him to pay double. Second offenders were sent to the Viet-Namese authorities for judgement, but this seldom happened. The paddy was golden and good, the houses well thatched, and the people happy. If the Viet-Namese were responsible for all this, good for them. Let them never forget that these tribesmen, so friendly and hospitable, were also stubborn, and proud, and – it was time for the ninth measure.

TWO

Border Incidents

CHAPTER SEVEN

A LONG WALK

I was sleeping on a bed in the *maison commune* at Plei Bon Mohr. Other tenants were forty unmarried members of the village, ranging from small boys to grown men. At night they lit fires, three and sometimes four. They crouched near the embers to keep warm, then fell asleep together in a heap. Apart from a loin-cloth they each had one other garment which served in turn as cloak, blanket, or satchel. I had been taking Paludrine against malaria, but never saw a single mosquito. There were plenty of flies, especially in the vicinity of the sacrificial pork. By wearing all my clothes in bed I could just keep warm. There was no incentive to get up early in the morning. I lay dreaming of jars and Bok Pim, while a crowd gathered outside the *maison commune*. This, I remembered, was the day of the much talked-about *commission*.

Siu-Rhing kept promising the *commission*, a kind of parade attended by the massed descendants of Bok Pim. Everything would be arranged in advance. He had also promised that I should see some gongs – not, alas, the gongs of Pim, but others very similar. A big crowd had gathered. It did not look as if we should start without Siu-Rhing, who was said to be washing. Meanwhile, Pim's family brought presents to my bedside – three eggs, the wing of a chicken, and delicious rice wrapped in jungle foliage. Inmate bachelors of the *maison commune* were going to give a display of gong-beating. Small, medium, and big, gongs and beaters came in many sizes, twenty in all. The gong-sticks were roots or small pieces of bamboo. The gongs were like English dinner-gongs. The gong-beaters began to form up on the loggia, while on the ground in front several hundred onlookers waited to see what would happen. Then they began their music. Starting in the bass, they worked up to treble with the precision of English bell-ringers. Nobody spoke. The sound of the gongs brought Pym from his bed. The music was sad. Not exactly a peal, not exactly a tune. The faces of the beaters were expressionless, calm, dignified. The sound of the gongs boomed out across the ricefields, past Pim's village and into the forest beyond.

There had to be an anti-climax. It came almost at once. Siu-Rhing was lurking near at hand. The gongs had sounded for only a few moments when he entered the scene, swaggering like a sergeant-major. The stars on his medal ribbons, the *Légion d'Honneur*, glinted in the early morning sun. Everything in his bearing declared him master of the situation, master of all the 25,000 tribesmen in the district of Ankhé. Young and old respected him, for they knew how many Viet-Minh Communists were shot dead from the barrel of his gun. The gongs stopped. Siu-Rhing mounted the loggia to make his speech. For the second time the villagers were told who I was, and where I was going. Bok Phinh was wearing a magnificent cloak I had never seen before. Bok Bieng was absent. Every now and then, Siu-Rhing pointed at me, and exclaimed: 'Bok Pym … Anglais. Bok Pym. Saigon–Qui-Nhon. Qui-Nhon–Binh-Dinh … Binh-Dinh … ' Then the recital of my journey. The descendants of Pim were summoned to form a special group on the right. Siu-Rhing organized them into a line of twenty or so right in front of the *maison commune*. As I took their photo, my eye was attracted once again by the racing curve of the thatched roof.

Events now took an unexpected and unwholesome turn. I was utterly dependent on Siu-Rhing. Without another interpreter at my side, I could not possibly flout his wishes. He embarked on a long speech, in which I recognized constant recurrence of the word 'Viet-Minh'. He told me he was summoning the former Viet-Minh collaborators, and wanted them to pose for their photo in the place recently vacated by Pim's family. This second group assembled rather slowly. Among them was a man whose head and hair reminded me of Peter Ustinov. He was half Bahnar, and half Jerai (a neighbouring tribe). During the Viet-Minh occupation he had been the collaborators' leader. Siu-Rhing lost no chance of reminding this character that he had been a traitor. But I noticed later that he walked about with a wily look on his face and drank at the jar of honour with the notables.

The allegedly pro-Viet-Minh group assembled, looking rather pleased with themselves. There was more delay while another of the ring-leaders was fetched from his house. When this was done, Siu-Rhing continued his speech. 'These men collaborated with the Viet-Minh,' he said. 'The watchword of our people is "Be Faithful". As a race, we must always keep faith. If the Viet-Minh come again, will these men be faithful?' A whisper ran through the assembly. The so-called pro-Communists conferred among themselves. After a moment, their leader, the Jerai half-breed, spoke in reply. 'It is uncertain,' he said. 'We have among our number some who would collaborate again if they had the chance.' I admired him for speaking so frankly, especially to Siu-Rhing, who, although a tribesman himself, was first and foremost the representative of South Viet-Nam's anti-Viet-Minh Government. 'If what you say is true,' replied Siu-Rhing, 'you must advise your followers on the most sensible course of action. Remember that among the Bahnars it is loyalty that counts. This is a warning which I give you for the last time. Take counsel among yourselves. Make no mistake.'

Then came the part I found distasteful. Siu-Rhing wanted a photo taken of the ex-collaborators. I suppose he thought that because I carried credentials from the Ministry of the Interior I would have to supply the Minister with photographs of anti-Government tribesmen. He insisted that I sully a portion of film with this row of gloomy-looking collaborators. I could not refuse him, nor did I shake the camera on purpose, but when the film was developed a few days later in Pleiku, all the pro-Communist faces were blurred. After a suitable pause, I stepped down into the crowd and handed the remains of my cigarettes and bonbons to Bok Phinh, who distributed them. The *commission* was over, and Pim's family took their leave.

Siu-Rhing was now free to take me on a tour of the village, including the big tombs of Mohr's wife and Rhing's own eldest son which I had not yet seen. He told me about a tribe living north of Plei Bon high up in the hills, who lived on honey and leaves and did not wash – the Mlum Bahnars. I found the Plei Bon villagers very unspoilt, far removed even from the Viet-Namese world on their doorstep. Though they were known as *montagnards,* this was a misnomer. Their ancestors probably lived in the coastal plain through which we had come, and were driven up into the hills by invading Chams and Annamites. At this moment of harvest-time, Plei Bon was a happy place. The paddy lay between the two villages like a golden shawl. The grain was not harvested, as in Cambodia, with a sickle, but grabbed from the top of its stalk and stuffed into a basket. All through one sunset I watched the tribesmen coming home from their fields with overflowing baskets strapped on their backs. The mountain rice had a tang all its own. Their alcohol stung the lips like rough cider. I had two presents to take home. The first was a crossbow with three arrows, offered by Bieng. It was well made, more robust, I thought, than those which are sold to tourists outside Angkor Wat. Bieng could hit a small leaf at fifteen yards range. I tried to equal his marksmanship, but the arrow flew high. The second present was a long eleven-inch pipe, not really for me but a wedding-present for my brother, who was due to be married in England very shortly. I wondered what was in store for me before I should deliver this pipe to its recipient. I had admired the Bahnar pipes, and was proud to have one in my possession. It was difficult, so they told me, to find a piece of wood with the necessary right-angled curve to make both stem and bowl without a join.

There were inevitable delays before departure – the preparation of food, finding guides, receiving gifts of salt and eggs. One of these eggs, was an antique in its own right, and, when it was opened, we found a chick hard-boiled. Four new guides were provided, one of whom I recognized from the second group at the *commission*. It was half-past seven – two hours lost on what turned out to be a most gruelling day's walk. I carried the rucksack myself. Cumbersome things, like the bow and arrow, were distributed among the tribesmen. Guides were at no time considered as porters, nor engaged to carry baggage, though they sometimes offered to do this. The first two hours were pleasant enough, a wooded track from Plei Bon to the road, then a short walk to a Viet-Namese village, where we bathed in cold mountain water and breakfasted on rice and eggs. Then we left the hills and set off across rolling moorland. When we next stopped beside another spring, one of the guides produced an old bird's nest. He ignited it by rubbing a supple piece of bark round a stick. It was the first time I had seen the Boy Scout's method in practice. I wondered if they were going to cook something. No – the fire was for lighting pipes and having a smoke.

The next landmark was a scar of red plough-soil recently claimed from the bush. There were rows of trim houses and vegetable gardens. A notice by the stream indicated which water was for drinking and which for washing. This was a new Viet-Namese settlement. My Bahnar friends looked apprehensive at being among so many Viet-Namese. They preferred to stay out on the dusty road while I drank some tea in a lean-to bistro. The Viet-Namese gathered round looking at us glumly. Never a smile, so we hurried on. The landscape changed to rolling down-land which reminded me of Wiltshire. Trim *monagnard*'s villages were sprinkled on the hillsides. In the twilight, my guides were reluctant to go in front. We closed into single file, and walked on steadily. We were never more glad to see the lights of a town than those of Pleiku. We had walked a real *montagnard*'s day, and had been on the road twelve hours. There were other lacerated feet besides mine. We entered the military camp that fringed the road into Pleiku. The eastern guardhouse was shut up, with sounds of revelry coming from within, and on the west side our arrival caused astonishment. I began my usual speech, but explanations were mercifully cut short by the arrival of the Head of Sûreté. He knew who I was apparently, and looked apprehensively at my blood-stained feet. We had been walking most of the day on the remains of the old road, number nineteen. This road, I remembered, had been a triumph of French road-building, like the Mandarin Route which once ran all the way up the coast of the China Sea. The Frenchmen who pioneered these roads dreamt about them in bed long after they had returned to France from dirty Indo-China (*sale Indochine*), as it was called by some. Such a dream is revealed in the words of a former French governor:

'*Le subtil esprit* [he writes] *de l'Annam se révèle à celui qui parcourt ces routes. Routes rouges serpentant au milieu de l'émeraude des rizières; routes grises du delta; routes sombres de la forêt épaisse où stridule le crissement metallique des cigales; routes parfumées par la floraison des lilas ou des frangipaniers, elles versent dans l'âme du voyageur le philtre mystérieux de cette Asie.*'

These were not exactly the feelings of our tribal procession as we stamped our way along the old French highway, and, as for our inquiries about an ancient Khmer road, they were completely fruitless. However, we would soon be in the zone where I hoped to find Neolithic tools. Meanwhile, it was pleasant to reach a place of some size, where there would be leisure to recuperate before continuing the journey.

CHAPTER EIGHT

TIGERS AHOY

This was Pleiku – pine-trees and cool nights in the heart of trop-ical Indo-China. Other hill-stations are higher and cooler but I have not yet been to them. Pleiku was a definite halting-point on the journey. Letters had to be written, and there was a Post Office, the last before Cambodia. The colour films which had missed me at Saigon were waiting to be collected from the airport. The Pleiku market was busy with tribesmen, who trooped in from neighbouring villages at first light. One man was bargaining to buy a blanket. Another was selling a chicken at the chemist's shop. By evening most of them had returned to their villages, some of which lay in the direction I hoped to travel.

The day was dominated by an interview with the provincial Governor, a dapper and gracious man. The Head of Sûreté was also present. By now we were good friends. The Governor had been well briefed. There was going to be a tussle. All I wanted was to continue my journey as approved by the Ministry of the Interior. The Governor was astonished by the phrase which read as follows: 'Pleiku to Cambodia on foot'. He delivered his prepared speech, which went something like this.

'I don't know if you will carry through this scheme. It is, you may know, dangerous to *walk* through these parts. More so, if you are a foreigner and are travelling alone. First, there are the tigers. Pleiku is famous for its tigers, more famous than anywhere else in Viet-Nam. Hardly a day passes without us filing a report on tribesmen being attacked by tigers. My Head of Sûreté can confirm this. He saw five all at once when he was out on patrol the other day.'

The Head of Sûreté nodded his agreement. I noticed later that he never referred to this particular incident, though usually tigers were his favourite subject of conversation. I felt he would prove a useful ally, especially as the Pleiku Sûreté was separate from the Governor and controlled by someone else far away in the south. The Governor continued: 'That is the first danger. I must warn you there is a second danger. When you get into the frontier region, there are, shall we say, certain elements beyond our control. When we make a patrol, they retreat into Cambodia or Laos. When we're not there, they come back. I can assure you – they are not *reasonable* people.' I wanted him to expatiate on these unreasonable elements. Were they Viet-Minh Communists, pirates, or what? 'If I knew,' he said, 'how many there are and who they are and where, I don't think they would exist for long.' Then we started a ninety-minute discussion, mostly about the reliability and degree of responsibility of tribesmen when acting as guides in the frontier region. 'In civilized countries like ours,' he said, 'we take certain responsibility for our guests.'

'Could one say,' I countered, 'that the odd dozen kilometres near the frontier do not really come within the definition of being civilized? You're not responsible for the conduct of a tiger, for example.' He replied, saying that touring cyclists who run up against bad conditions put their bikes on a lorry and continue afterwards as best they can. This gave me the opening I wanted. He had previously described the route as very overgrown with bamboo and impassable even for a jeep. 'Only a pedestrian can make it,' I said. 'Your comparison does not hold good. No jeep, let alone a lorry, can pass along this track.'

A bleak fact had to be admitted. The Viet-Namese–Cambodian frontier was closed. Also, the road number nineteen which once linked the two countries at this point was not being used on either side of the border. I tried drawing a historical sketch of the district, emphasizing what the early French explorers had achieved under difficult conditions. I pointed out that the number of tigers had been diminishing during the last eighty years. The Governor laughed.

'Honestly,' he said, 'I can't tell you if there are more or less tigers here today than there were fifty years ago. I do know that my Head of Sûreté saw five in a bunch, and that we have had more than a hundred incidents in the last twelve months.'

The interview was a setback. I did not know if the police would prevent my leaving Pleiku for the frontier, or whether they would merely refrain from helping. It was too late in the day to start looking for guides, so I went to bed in low spirits. The next day started with an attempt to re-establish cordial relations with the Head of Sûreté, who had been a little cool since my interview with the Governor. This was not difficult, for he was also my host, and looked after me very well in his little house. In the morning I went down to the market, and tried to find guides to go with me to Cambodia. The schoolmaster from Pim's village had arrived to do some shopping. There were other tribesmen who recognized us from the road, and spoke cordially. After the Governor's statement that the frontier was overgrown, I had to face the possibility of clearing a way through. For this a weapon was essential. I wanted the kind of sabre which I had seen tribesmen carrying. There were none on sale at the market. The nearest was a rough-looking sickle with a long wooden handle. It was cheap and shoddy, but I had to have something, and it looked as if it would cut bamboo. Later I met a tribesman who owned two sabres.

He worked for an evangelical Christian mission, and was very willing to sell me what I wanted. The sabre, which then changed hands, was smaller than some I had seen, but the proportions between blade and handle were pleasing. It was light, convenient, and the blade frighteningly sharp. I resold the useless sickle at a small loss, and returned home the proud owner of a sabre. Then I remembered that I was not completely unarmed. I always had the bow and arrow presented by Pim's grandson, Bieng, but this would be no use for clearing a blocked frontier. Now it seemed that the Viet-Namese were not going to stop me leaving Pleiku, so I planned the journey ahead. All my plans depended on the police letting me continue. The Head of Sûreté gave me sealed letters of introduction, but I was not sure what he was planning to do when I reached a place called Cuty which had a police-post. He gave me no introductory letters for anywhere beyond this post.

Just before I started out, the Head of Sûreté tried a new, and more subtle, approach to try told discourage me from continuing. 'Like to see a photo of a tiger I shot?' he said casually, and produced a snap of himself beside the head of what seemed to be the biggest tiger in South-East Asia. Three metres long, it had been shot at eight o'clock in the morning near the Mang Yang pass. 'I hope to find some more tigers like that,' he said, and then with emphasis, 'near the police-post at Cuty.'

A good book about Indo-China, which mentions Cuty, is Norman Lewis's *A Dragon Apparent*. After making my own journey I read this book and discovered that we must have met some of the same people although seven years separated our journeys. Norman Lewis failed to do in wartime what I was attempting in peace. He was turned back at the police-post of Cuty. Would my fate be the same? I had so far been unsuccessful

85

in my search for traces of the ancient Khmer road, though finding Pim's village was something achieved. My journey was not yet two weeks old.

I left Pleiku on the same road number nineteen, still moving westwards. Search for a guide was soon successful, and my new companion put himself in my good books at once by leaving the road and setting off along a tribesman's path towards his village. A cool breeze blew across the open downland. Occasionally, the path descended sharply to a stream or marsh. We had now left the Bahnar tribal areas, and entered a Jerai district (see Fig. 1, p. 33). Stops were made at four Jerai villages. At each the guides resigned and handed me over to a friend or relation. It was hard to make oneself understood, but I picked up a few words of the language. The Jerai word for 'horse' sounded like the Cambodian sell. Villages were spick and span, houses evenly spaced with firewood beneath, everything swept tidily. The inside of a Jerai house consists of a long room with bamboo shelves. We settled in one of these at midday and were offered food by the head of the village. This was a typical Jerai meal of cold rice, salt, and something green and hard, which was neither fruit nor vegetable. I was hungry and ate greedily. It was a quick change from the civilized breakfast of butter and rolls at Pleiku.

Each new guide walked a little faster than the last, or so it seemed. Tigers were uppermost in my mind. I recalled a certain engraving of Henri Mouhot, showing him sitting with his gun beside a blazing fire in the middle of the jungle. By mid-afternoon a pungent smell told me we were approaching a tea plantation. The guides led me round the back to the plantation labour village, where a policeman greeted us genially. He seemed amiable, and turned out to be half Cambodian, and half Viet-Namese. The plantation was managed by Frenchmen, the last

Europeans I would see for some time to come. Tigers dominated the conversation. The French were being treated like tribesmen in the matter of firearms. Only one of the four, a seasoned big-game hunter, was allowed by the Viet-Namese to carry a gun. Tigers came into the plantation garden, and had once invaded the kitchen looking for scraps. B, the hunter, turned out to be a useful source of information about the road ahead.

Two months earlier, apparently, there had been a double frontier incident. Patrols had gone out from each side and collected hostages. The victims were said to have been taken into Cambodia and Viet-Nam respectively, where they were believed to have languished and died. B explained that the chief difficulty would be persuading the tribesmen to lead me into Cambodia, especially if the Viet-Namese tried to stop us leaving.

'What about the state of the track?' I asked. 'Is it very overgrown?'

Overgrown was a polite word for blocked. The Cambodians, suspecting Viet-Namese wood-cutters were pilfering on Cambodian soil, had deliberately blocked the frontier with tree-trunks. If I had been travelling by jeep, this would have been the end of the journey. But I was not in a jeep, I was on foot. There were said to be plenty of good paths through the hills. A village called Plei Lom Yadon was suggested as a good place to make for. It lay somewhat to the south of the blocked road number nineteen. The tribesmen in this region did not know themselves just where the frontier ran. They would come down on the wrong side to buy and sell their produce, and return the way they had come. I had a pleasant evening with the plantation staff, ending with a hot bath, my second since leaving England. Then I retired to sleeping-quarters in the police-station, splendid except that when all the windows and doors were bolted and barred very little air could get in. Instead, smoke from a kitchen next door, where there was no proper chimney, filtered over the partition. Late at night the kitchen fire died down, and I fell asleep as the smoke decreased.

CHAPTER NINE

FULL MOON AT CUTY

The new guides were Viet-Namese, not tribesmen. We left the plantation along forest paths, but soon emerged on to the road number nineteen for half a day's walk which brought us to a village near an army camp. I made friends with the Government's Head of Sector – a tribesman who was responsible for recruiting tribal labour squads. I asked about paths to Lom Yadou, and he confirmed that these paths existed. If all went well, he said, I should be able to find guides at Cuty who would take me to Lom Yadou, which was the other side of the frontier in Cambodia. He advised us to stay the night at his village and go on to Cuty the next day. The guides invited me to lunch with some friends, and we had rice and soup made from tasteless red vegetables. It was served in a small room where the only piece of furniture besides table and chairs was an altar. There were two pictures on the altar – portrait (head and shoulders only) of President Ngo Dinh Diem and Jesus Christ – about the same size.

The afternoon was spent visiting a tribal village and inquiring about possible remains of the ancient Khmer road. One of the tribesmen was wearing black Viet-Namese-style garments. At first I mistook his nationality. He turned out to be a Jerai working for a Viet-Namese Government development scheme. I asked about 'development' and he said it consisted of giving advice to the villagers.

'What kind of advice?' I asked.

'Keeping the village well swept,' he replied. 'How to plant

vegetables, use chopsticks and so on.'

'Why use chopsticks?' I asked. By now I was accustomed to using fingers at a *montagnard* meal.

'Hygiene,' replied the Development Officer briskly. 'Working in the fields, the hands get dirty.' I held my peace.

A stream ran between the Viet-Namese and tribal villages. Along the banks there were newly cultivated vegetable gardens. 'Who has the right to plant vegetables here?' I asked. 'You must understand,' he replied, 'that the tribespeople have not yet learned *how* to plant. That is the reason why you don't see them here.' The gardens were all Viet-Namese owned. There was a single tribesman working there, a healthy-looking chap. 'If he works for a year,' said my friend, 'he can buy a bicycle. Viet-Namese hire him to do their work.'

Our reception in the tribal village was influenced by the presence of my Viet-Namese guides, who had come with me that morning from the plantation. I asked the villagers some questions. They had never heard of the Khmers or the Chams. They had never seen brick or stone ruins anywhere in the neighbouring forest, nothing which looked anything like a stone bridge or rest-house. I always hoped to find a bridge or rest-house, for the existence of either in this region would indubitably establish the presence of an ancient Khmer road from Angkor to the coast. These villages were all on the beaten track, to which I had to cling as long as I remained in Viet-Nam. It was an area well-known to the French in their time, and I had little chance of finding anything useful. It was, however, a good opportunity of learning about the tribesmen. They said their god lived in the sky, and had no house on earth at all, not even in the deepest jungle.

'Why,' I asked, 'do you beat gongs at festivals?'

'We beat them,' they answered, 'because we like the noise, and it makes everyone happy.'

Then there was an awkward pause when they asked if I wanted to give the village any 'advice'. I supposed that this particular village was used to visiting firemen, like myself, I declined the offer, while the guides explained to the people what little they knew about me. One phrase kept recurring. It could be rendered into English, so I gathered, as follows: 'President Ngo Dinh Diem has sent this Englishman to have a look at your village. Mind you behave properly while he's here.'

Our party set out for Cuty six strong. The road began to descend. After crossing one or two streams I remembered that these must be tributaries of the Sre Pok, a large eastern affluent of the River Mekong. That meant we were getting nearer Cambodia.

The grass was high on both sides, the forest thick. Sometimes we heard the rustle of an animal moving, but saw nothing, not even a green snake.

This was my second day with the two Viet-Namese from the plantation. They had thawed considerably. One of them was always making jokes. When we stopped for lunch in a tribal village, he seized a piece of wood and chopped it into four pairs of chopsticks. The tribesmen arranged fresh green leaves in the shape of trays, then disposed a mountain of freshly-cooked rice. They watched inquisitively, to see us use our newly made chopsticks. This, I realized, was part of their 'Viet-Namization'. The guides also made cups and plates from banana leaves so that no grain of rice was wasted. There were several kinds of unsavoury vegetable soup. The rice tasted good as usual. The second guide, who could speak the Jerai language, was rather surly. He felt he had to establish his Viet-Namese authority over the tribesmen, or else he would lose face. The village was trim like the others. Goats, pigs and poultry scratched round, good bait for a tiger.

As we continued our journey, there were occasional views of the forest, now less thick. The plateau slopes gradually down from here to the banks of the River Mekong (see Fig. 1, p. 33). There would be no more passes, I hoped. In the afternoon we reached Cuty, where the Police-chief gave us a cordial welcome. After listening to explanations from the plantation guides, one of whom worked in the Sûreté, he said he would make arrangements to get me into Cambodia. I could feel in my pocket the letter of recommendation from the Head of Sûreté at Plan. I had no idea of its contents, but suspected it would tell the man at Cuty not to let me go forward. This was guesswork. I never found out what was in the letter. Anyway, I decided to hold it in reserve. It was advantageous to prefabricate an 'umbrella' for the Viet-Namese. In case of accident, I could be held responsible by them 'for failing to deliver a letter concerning the Government's arrangements for his protection'. The police who had been so friendly would not have to take the blame.

The reader will remember that the search for Neolithic tools was a secondary purpose of my journey. The original finds had been made at the plantation near Pleiku. An enterprising member of the plantation staff had collected some Neolithic tools, which were later classified by an expert. The tools had come to light during some construction work which had now finished. Their collector had returned to France with T.B. I was now in an area west of the plantation, so when our party reached Cuty I thought the time was ripe to begin my search. I had no sooner started out when a shout attracted our attention from the other end of the village.

'Tiger.'

It was dead already. The Head of Sûreté had said Cuty was the tigers' stronghold, and his words proved true. The tigress, as she was, measured nine feet from nose to tip of tail. She was lean, and must have been hungry. The villagers had killed her that morning at a hamlet we had passed on our way. There had been a full-dress tiger-hunt. Thirty hunters had given chase with lances and bows and arrows. I arrived on the scene just before Viet-Namese merchants flayed the skin. The beast was already sold for three thousand five hundred piastres (about £35). This was the *prix fixe* for the neighbourhood. The most valuable part was the skeleton. The bones would fetch a good price, and be sold as medicine in the big cities. The merchants were willing to sell the skin, but none of them knew how to cure it properly. The decaying skin of a tigress was not, I decided, a suitable object to be added to my luggage for the march into Cambodia. The tiger-meat was being sold for eating, Cambodian Buddhist monks are not allowed to eat tiger, but there were no such restrictions at Cuty. Many of the Viet-Namese bought a kilogram or two. There was a certain repugnance to overcome before the first taste. I sampled a grilled tiger-steak that evening, and found it most delicious. According to the locals the tigers were specially hungry at the end of the rainy season. They often came to the villages for goats and hens. Miss Tigress – she was not an old hand – had come once too often.

There was a spate of tiger stories. Two nights earlier the Cuty schoolchildren had heard something tapping at the dormitory window. One of them went outside with a lantern and met a large tiger. The tiger ran away, but a few minutes later came back and began scratching up earth from under the bamboo door. The walls were so flimsy that there was danger the tiger would break in and attack before the alarm could be given. The children sat up all night, stoking fires to frighten away the attacker. It was a pity that these Jerai schoolchildren could not be liberated from fear of tigers in the night. But the family firearms had been confiscated.

The schoolmaster's predecessor had found a Neolithic axe-head in the forest, which I was allowed to take away. This was evidence that the Neolithic finds at the plantation were not purely local. The tool itself was disfigured with scratch-marks. Powder, scratched from a thunder-axe, as they are called, was said by the Jerai to be effective against headaches. When I had been given this axe-head, I was shown the tribal school. The buildings were in good repair, but the pupils disinclined to work. One-sixth of them were permanently absent – presumably in their villages. The principal subject taught was the Viet-Namese language, of which the Jerai teachers did not sometimes have more than a superficial knowledge. This was part of 'Viet-Namization'. Formerly, I heard, the tribal children had a class of 'practical studies' – learning how to plant produce and rear livestock. It had been discontinued, and no reason given. It was bad luck that these lads and lasses in loin-cloths should not be learning something of immediate practical value in a tribal village.

In the evening I was invited by the tribal schoolmaster to a funeral fête in a nearby village. A twenty-day-old baby had died that morning about the same time as the tigress met her end. The village was one kilometre's distance, on the other side of a valley. The path was infested with large black ants, whose bites were most painful. It was, unexpectedly, a night to remember, for the village stood on the slope of a hill, and, in front, the full moon was only just beginning to wane. The funeral was due to last several days, though the family was not rich. There were two parts – before the burial and after. The programme was familiar – gongs, jars and a sacrificed animal.

When we arrived, the bachelors were leading an anti-clockwise procession round the dead child's house, beating gongs with the same sad cadence I had heard at Pim's village. Then the young girls of the village gathered in a secluded place and tied white kerchiefs round their heads. Linking arms, shoulder to shoulder, they formed a giant conga and danced round the house. A dozen steps forward, then a few steps back. Always they progressed a little, in the opposite direction to the men. Between the female conga and the house the young men continued to move anti-clockwise, beating gongs all the time. Sometimes the two moving circles closed together till there was hardly any space between men and women. A youth detached himself from the gong-beaters and joined on to the female conga, shouting for joy. The women ranged according to height. Taller girls led. At the end of the line there were six-year-olds and infants. They danced joyously, laughing if anyone missed a step. Sometimes they clapped their hands to beat out the time. Once they reversed positions so that everyone faced outwards with backs to the house of the dead.

We did a courtesy round of jars, and demolished seven measures each. The liquor was not so strong as at Pim's village. The schoolmaster went on drinking till dawn, and was very much the worse for wear the next day.

CHAPTER TEN

BLOCKED FRONTIER

The Viet-Namese policeman was annoyed when I arrived back late from the tribal feast. Already in bed, he said gruffly: 'You won't be able to go to Cambodia tomorrow. There are no tribal guides available.' I was happy to spend another day at Cuty, where the people were so friendly. But there was something ominous in the policeman's words. I hoped the difficulties would solve themselves in time. In these circumstances it seemed wise now to let the policeman have my letter of introduction from Pleiku. I had omitted to deliver it the day before. A couple of hours later the Head of Sûreté arrived in person, He had driven out from Pleiku by jeep and was dressed in spotless khaki. We exchanged the latest tiger news, then he said: 'I just came to learn your decision.' I told him briskly that I wished to proceed. The old arguments were canvassed and new ones given a first airing. The Sûreté man was going up towards the frontier on a tour of inspection. I suggested that I join him for the ride on condition that he brought me back to Cuty, where I could continue my walk from the place I had left off. On the way, we worked out a new plan. I was to sign an engagement exonerating the Viet-Namese Government from all responsibility once I was over the frontier, The Head of Sûreté left me to prepare the exact wording. I wondered what to write, as we drove along. If I came to a bad end, this document would become rather important to my family, the Press, the Consul, and so on.

The road towards the frontier was not as deserted as people tried to persuade me. A good many tribesmen were going to and from the villages. The next police-post was a surprise. I expected a hamlet even tinier than Cuty. Instead, there was a vast expanse of recently cleared jungle, hundreds of new houses, and scores of Viet-Namese burning forest debris. It had all happened in less than a year. The colonizers here were not political refugees from North Viet-Nam, but resettled farmers whose land in the coastal strip was insufficient or unfertile. The earth looked red and rich. I learnt later that some of the first settlers here found life extremely hard. A few fell ill and died, while others returned home. The project appeared to have been saved by President Ngo Dinh Diem, who made a visit in person and sent his own doctor to look after the settlers' health. We discussed the possibilities of my getting into Cambodia via the village of Lom Yadou. The replies were guarded. 'All we can say,' they said, 'is that we do not advise you to go to Lom Yadou.' According to rumours in Cuty, Lom Yadou had been the scene of a recent Viet-Namese foray on to Cambodian territory. It was understandable that anyone emerging there from Viet-Nam would receive a cool reception. Another rumour said that a party of thirty Viet-Minh Communists had recently descended on a nearby village to buy food. Government patrols had given chase without catching anyone.

'You know,' said the Head of Sûreté, 'this frontier is closed. The Cambodians have blocked it with trees.' After more discussion he said he would arrange for an escort of tribesmen who would be told to take me through the jungle to the nearest Cambodian post. For my part I had to sign the engagement we had already discussed. As we drove back to Cuty I decided that formality should be the keynote of this document, which I thereupon drafted, using my unimpressive French as a common language. The last paragraph said that when the Viet-Namese had taken me to the limits of their country I would deliver them a letter. This letter, which I did not propose writing till the actual moment, would be addressed to the British Vice-Consul in Saigon. It would say that I had departed, safely or otherwise, into Cambodia. The Head of Sûreté consulted some notes of his own, and said he was satisfied with the wording I had used. I could imagine him throwing it down with a flourish on the Governor's desk.

When the engagement was signed and stamped, I thought all would now be plain sailing. The next morning started with an anticlimax – instead of the great departure for the Cambodian frontier, none of the previous day's arrangements seemed to be working. There was no sign of my tribal escort. The tribal Head of Sector appeared – I had first met him several days before. 'We can't abandon you on the frontier,' he said. 'Let me find you some of my partisans to go the whole way. I'll write them a laissez-passer myself.' This opened up new vistas. Did the Jerai tribesmen have their own system of papers and passes working independently of the Cambodian and Viet-Namese Governments? The Head of Sector seemed an unlikely person to wield such power. The idea of going with his partisans appealed very much. He was a big bear-like man who could speak tolerable French. I tried to hold him to his word, but off he went, and that was the last I saw of him.

Meanwhile I was losing confidence in the local police. My host's contact with tribesmen took place exclusively through Viet-Namese interpreters. Escorts which he ordered from surrounding hamlets failed to turn up – twice. One of the Cuty merchants had a Land-Rover, so we went out to visit some villages. The wheels were not properly connected to the steering-wheel. The vehicle swayed down a narrow track, bouncing off tree-stumps and rocking dangerously up grassy banks. The villages were typical. Their maisons communes had beautiful circular doorways with jaw-bones of oxen hanging up inside. The merchant went round houses bartering for sacks of rice. My policeman sat tight, occasionally making notes on a scrap of paper. At midday there seemed to have been no progress, although he had said he was trying to recruit an escort. 'Leave it to us,' he assured me. 'Your mountain guides will come tonight. It is certain.' He told me the name of their village. Unfortunately for him, I knew about this village already. The entire male population had gone on a two-day deer-hunt together with inhabitants from three other neighbouring villages. I prepared to wait another night at Cuty, if necessary.

That afternoon I returned to the tribal burial feast, which had moved from the hillside village to a cemetery in the valley. There was a shaded clearing beneath the trees. A few tribesmen were gossiping round a plate of vegetable mash and the inevitable jar. We occupied the time finding words common to both the Jerai and Cambodian languages, e.g. sword, shirt, trousers, horse. In the evening there was another fête. The schoolmaster had been having nightmares about his son, who was away at school. He dreamt that the boy was being beaten with staves like an ox. The school had given special permission for the son to come home. The aim of the fete was to chase away the bad spirit which had caused the dream. A pig was sacrificed and three jars broached. One of them was brewed with banana mixed into the rice. It was sweetly appetizing and very alcoholic. We moved round the jars in turn listening to, and telling stories.

In this district, they said, there was a mysterious tribesman who used to accost travellers on the road and then disappear. He would reappear farther on transformed into a tiger with all the information he needed to make a successful kill. The story was said to originate from a tiger once killed in this region and found to have a gold tooth. The tribesmen declared that only humans have gold teeth. Therefore, the tiger must have been a human in disguise. The schoolmaster complained that the tribesmen round Cuty were very different from those at his own home, though both were called Jerai. At Cuty they reduced tribal life to its lowest terms – field, jar, jar, field. There was no spontaneous movement for improving conditions – nothing. Here was one people, it seemed, as yet untouched by the better-and-more doctrine.

The next morning I had a pre-dawn breakfast of boiled eggs and coffee, and when no tribal guides materialized I prepared to take the road alone for the first time. Tired of delays, I was afraid that if I did not show my determination to move, the Viet-Namese might think I was losing heart, and even be prepared to give up the journey. I had no intention of giving up the journey, but was looking forward to the moment when I would enter Cambodia and forests full of ancient Khmer remains. Normally I distributed certain pieces of equipment, such as the bow and arrow, to my companions. Now there was no option but to pack everything into one awkward bundle, with the bow and arrow strapped on the top. The sun was rising fast, and my road lay to the west. Clasping my sabre in the right hand, I set off. This, I decided afterwards, was the most serio-comic moment of the whole journey comic for obvious reasons, and serious because there existed a real danger from tigers. After a few minutes I was pursued by a Viet-Namese with entreaties and promises which I had to ignore. Ten minutes later I was caught up by the head policeman. He was riding a bicycle, and still wearing his pyjamas. He implored me to return and said the guides would be ready in one hour's time. Three times he had promised guides. Three times they had failed to turn up, so I politely declined the offer to delay my departure, and strode off again into the west. Glancing back, I saw a pyjamaed figure mount his bicycle sadly and pedal slowly back over the hill to Cuty. He had been an excellent host. I was treating him badly.

It was the ideal time of day for walking. I kept an eye on the long grass, and fingered my sabre. Everything seemed quiet – the tiger's hour. After an hour or so, two cyclists caught me up and stayed the rest of the way to the frontier settlement. Here I found a sergeant in command. By the time we had discussed the situation over a glass of tea, there were some new arrivals. Who should they be but three specially appointed tribal guides? The police-chief at Cuty had been as good as his word. The guides had come hot-foot after me, but never caught up. These, surely, were the three tribesmen who would lead me into Cambodia. They were young, smiling, and looked very fit. Departure was fixed for five o'clock the next morning.

In the afternoon the Sergeant lent me a very old soldier, the kind who in England is allowed to come on parade wearing a 1940 forage cap. We went off together to look for Neolithic tools. There was so much digging going on at the new settlement that our chances of finding something were fair. After speaking to one or two of the workers, my guide was directed down the valley to a stream, said to be a favourite haunt of tigers. We shouldered our arms, he his sten-gun and I my sabre. The old soldier waded into the water as if he'd been looking for Neolithic axe-heads all his life. Perhaps he thought we were looking for gold. No tools, no tigers.

Returning to the settlement we found the hitherto-absent officer commanding had returned from leave. He was an interesting fellow, a real mountain-dwelling tribesman, whose tribe lived on the Viet-Namese–Chinese border, that is, in the Communist territory of North Viet-Nam (see Map A). Many of his countrymen had come south as refugees from Communism and were now living and working on the plateau. The return of the C.O. was a shock and surprise to the tribal soldiers at the settlement. One of them appeared in front of the house, half-drunk. He waved a hand and tried to make an incoherent salute, which ended in his being hurried away to the guardroom. 'They're quite hopeless,' said the Lieutenant, 'if you let them get at their jars. This place used to be virgin jungle. That was eight months ago when I first arrived. Work began at the beginning of the rainy season. Yes, it was difficult. Some of the settlers caught malaria, not many!'

By chance, the morrow was the exact date on which I had told the British Vice-Consul in Saigon that I hoped to leave Viet-Nam. In eighteen days I had received a multitude of impressions which did not give a balanced picture of the country. I wanted to do the same thing in North Viet-Nam, then settle down to learn the language before travelling again. As for Cambodia, I was already on the fourth or fifth lap. I had learnt the language and studied a number of things that interested me. Time would show whether my first impressions of Viet-Nam were right. It was bad luck on friendly hosts that I had not been able to do their country justice. On this last evening in Viet-Nam, I thought back over the journey. I was anxious about the future of the tribes – Pim's people and the Jerais. I had seen that South Viet-Nam was tackling the problem with energy. How about Communist North Viet-Nam? But now it was time to leave Viet-Nam and set off for the Viet-Namese–Cambodian frontier, which I have chosen to call 'the sugar-palm curtain'.

CHAPTER ELEVEN

SUGAR-PALM CURTAIN

Before dawn the valley near the frontier was echoing with the cries of the settlers. Every morning they did half an hour's physical jerks before starting on communal tasks. It was an impressive sight. Our party numbered nine. Besides my three tribal guides from Cuty, there was a military escort comprising a tribal sergeant and four armed tribal soldiers. After crossing a waterfall, our way was barred by wooded hills. As we climbed higher, the wood turned to forest and then jungle. The path was sinuous and overgrown with shrubs and young bamboo. This was the dry season, but there were plenty of leeches. I yearned for that office of an old London publisher where I had once spent so many dusty hours. Which was worse, the blood-sucking leech or the perpetual buzz of a managing director's intercom? After an hour and a half we reached a deserted jungle ricefield. From there, another forty minutes took us to a tiny village. The grain was golden and ready to be cut. We stopped for a big meal of fresh rice and half-cooked meat. I retrieved some crumpled pieces of paper from my rucksack, and wrote the letter which our Sergeant would bear through the jungle back to the frontier, and thence to the British Vice-Consul in Saigon.

Although there was not a sugar-palm in sight, we were now poised on what I have been calling 'the sugar-palm curtain'. I drag in the sugar-palms here because they are a feature of the landscape along the Viet-Namese–Cambodian frontier at the regular place for crossing. I was crossing at an irregular place, which is perhaps why the Viet-Namese tried to discourage me. At the time of this journey the regular frontier between South Viet-Nam and Cambodia, far away in the south, was open. As you drive along the good road which approaches this frontier from Saigon, you first traverse a desolate plain – the haunt of rebels in wartime days – this is South Viet-Nam. When you see a horizon dotted with sugar-palm trees you know that you are about to enter Cambodia. The sugar-palms on this frontier are most striking. We know iron, and bamboo curtains, but not sugar-palm curtains. At the time of my journey the Chinese and Viet-Namese minorities of neutral Cambodia were suspected by South Viet-Nam of having pro-Communist sympathies. When they went on visits to anti-Communist South Viet-Nam, their families feared they might not see them return. So to some travellers the Viet-Namese–Cambodian frontier seemed like a curtain – the sugar-palm curtain.

This was the point at which our military escort could go no farther. However, they said cheerfully that a Viet-Namese patrol, sixty strong, had been absent from camp for a week. We might meet them inside Cambodia. I hoped not. I was additionally anxious, for we were now heading for Lom Yadou, the village which the Sûreté had specially advised us to avoid. The soldiers smiled as they watched our party, now reduced to four, weave its way through the golden paddy and on up the hill. None of us had firearms. Two of the guides carried Union Jacks. The third had a Buddhist flag which I hoped would be respected by Cambodian marksmen along the frontier, if we should meet any. In the first deserted ricefield the guides missed the way. We tramped round in the blazing sun and eventually found a path which led back into the forest. Thirty minutes brought us to another patch of abandoned rice. There were wild banana-trees and bright scarlet flowers. Then we crossed a stream. Was this the Cambodian frontier? Another thirty minutes in the wood brought us to a bigger stream, where a young Jerai girl was bathing naked near some fish-traps. Her ears had recently been pierced. The lobes contained large, knobbly cylinders of wood to keep them stretched.

We re-entered the forest. After an hour or more, the guides admitted that they did not know which way they were going. They said we had by-passed Lom Yadou. The paths separated and joined. Sometimes the guides stopped and studied the way the grass was lying, or to look at a piece of earth, freshly trodden, whether by man or beast I did not know. Then we would turn off to right or left, sometimes choosing the more overgrown path of the two. I could tell from the sun that we were heading north-west – the direction of Cambodia. Once we emerged on to a wooded spur, where the guides took a terrific turn backwards and began walking east. I said nothing. The track gradually straightened out and forty minutes later we were heading due west. Then we came to a mountain stream, almost a river, with a deep pool for swimming and a pleasant waterfall. As we continued through this no-man's-land, there were two more abandoned rice-fields, a river, a stream, then a patch of inhabited paddy surrounded by trees. An old woman was sitting there eating some cold rice. While we were talking, a single shot sounded somewhere to the north. Was that the Viet-Namese patrol? I prayed we would not meet them, or their opposite numbers from Cambodia.

At a quarter-past three in the afternoon we reached a sizeable village. Nearly every inhabitant was suffering from skin diseases, and one old man had an enormous sore on his thigh. I did what I could for him with bandages and ointment. I did not want to help them too much. A false rumour would spread before me that a French doctor was visiting the villages. This could only lead to disappointment, and even hostility. None of them here could speak Cambodian, but they seemed to understand the words: 'Do you speak Cambodian?' Two more guides were added to the party. They led us through a muddy pool and a swamp. Just before dark we reached a big village. I heard a sound like music to the ears – a Jerai tribesman who spoke Cambodian.

'Elder brother,' he said. 'Where are you going?'

'I'm going west,' I replied.

North, south, east, west. This is the traditional answer to the question 'Where are you going?', used by Cambodians wherever they greet each other whether in town or country. The tribesmen addressed me as 'elder brother' – a mark of respect on the friendliest level. I was really glad to be entering Cambodia, a country which I already knew well, and where I could make myself understood in the local language. From this moment onwards the journey became more tranquil, the contacts with villagers less exhausting, and the daily harvest of travellers' tales infinitely rewarding.

Our reception at this first village inside Cambodia was excellent, more so because the chief guide found he was among relations and friends. After long years of absence a family reunion took place between him and his uncle. The uncle presented me with a speckled hen. It was killed for supper and payment refused. The reader must remember that the Jerai tribal area straddles the Viet-Namese–Cambodian frontier, which as far as the tribesmen are concerned is an arbitrary division. My guides unwrapped three soiled tunics made of dingy khaki, which they offered for sale. Nobody wanted to buy, so we lay down exhausted and went to sleep. Smoke from the internal fires seeped across the long wood cabin protecting us from the sharp chill of dawn. I was not sure if difficulties were now over. What sort of reception would I find at the Cambodian frontier-post? A single foreigner emerging on foot from a closed Viet-Namese frontier was severe poison to offer any Cambodian. There was also the problem of getting to Stung-Treng through country which was said to be just as full of tigers as that through which we had already passed. We left the village at crack of dawn, and soon reached another where the houses seemed longer and more stately. The village square was surrounded by 'long houses', if one may so call them without misusing the term. One was being used as a maison commune. The first letter of the Cambodian alphabet was written eighteen times on the rafters. Ah, I thought, 'Cambodianization'. We greedily demolished a meal of rice and bad eggs. This was where the three tribal guides from Viet-Nam decided they would turn back. I was deeply grateful to them for coming far into Cambodian territory at their own personal risk. It was our good luck that so far there had been absolutely no sign of the Cambodian Army or police. We were in an unpoliced Jerai tribal area. Once again my guides exhibited their old khaki tunics. This time there was no difficulty in exchanging them for three handsome-looking sabres. Mental arithmetic told me that the deal was much to their advantage. Both parties were content, however, and sat together talking and joking. The sabres, I guessed, would end up in the market at Pleiku – the age-old way in which goods from Laos were still finding their way through Cambodia into South Viet-Nam.

Where was I? The map was not much help. We were entering an area which had not been properly mapped at all. Information had been culled from old documents, e.g., the itineraries of people like myself. The villagers knew where the Cambodian frontier-post was, so we set off hopefully north-west. Before twelve o'clock fifteen different guides had been employed. They organized relays from one village to the next. Arrival at a village followed a pattern. We walked to the middle of the square, where there was usually a maison commune. Here we could sit in the shade while new guides prepared themselves for the road. I thought I recognized one or two typical Cambodian-looking faces, although this was still a jerai tribal area. The women reminded me of Laotians. There was another marsh to cross outside the next village. It was traversed by a series of narrow log foot-bridges. They would have been easy to cross normally, but carrying the fifteen-kilo rucksack, it was difficult to balance and avoid falling into the stinking pit.

New guides led off at right angles to a straight grass track, which looked as if it might go somewhere. We stopped to rest in a deserted ricefield where a jerai couple, as old as the hills, were living off some wild-looking rice. Their tumbledown shack was full of food, which they offered hospitably – cucumbers, tobacco, and slices of scorched pumpkin. Then we plunged into almost impenetrable jungle. Grasses and plants met overhead, making us crouch down and burrow through the tunnel which had once been a path. Then came brambles and a bamboo thicket. My Cambodian sleeping-mat, strapped to the bottom of the rucksack, was too wide for the path. Its fibres were continually caught up with thorns. By the end of the day they were frayed and torn. At the next hamlet the only inhabitants were two old women, who were kind enough to cook up some of the rice I had brought from Viet-Nam. It was late in the afternoon before new guides appeared. They were courteous, and made me a present of five bantam's eggs. After negotiating another overgrown path, we arrived full of thorns in yet another village, where I decided to stop for the night. Another meal was served – rice, made appetizing by the addition of grilled pig's fat in chunks. A day had passed without our reaching the Cambodian frontier-post. The seventeen guides had followed a trail from village to village by circuitous paths. The night was passed comfortably beside the embers of a dying fire. The jerai – they called themselves jerai, but the language was already different – sat round in a group, smoking their long pipes and swigging savoury water from shapely black gourds.

The next morning I had to change guides continuously till an extra bonus persuaded two young tribesmen to stay till we reached our destination. About nine o'clock we saw a cluster of thatched roofs and welcome signs of a banana grove. This was the Cambodian frontier-post of Bokeo reached at last. It had taken fifty hours to get through the sugar-palm curtain. We were soon walking between a double row of Chinese shops, then started a climb up to what looked like the Governor's house. Behind us there was another hill with a Buddhist monastery on it. There were scenes of great activity. Three companies of tribal recruits were drilling on a hillside parade-ground. The sentry let us through a gate. As we crossed the forecourt a sharp command rapped out.

'Drop your luggage.'

The voice spoke in French. I could not see where it came from. We tried to advance. There was more shouting: 'Drop that sabre. Stay where you are.' Humbled before the gaze of three hundred tribesmen and Cambodians, I let my sabre slip to the ground. The two guides stood their ground with me, but we were too tired to shout back at the unseen questioner. I felt that all three of us might well be near the inside of a Cambodian gaol.

THREE

Into Cambodia

CHAPTER TWELVE

BOKEO

Was I the first Englishman to arrive in Cambodia by this uncon-
ventional route? It was hardly surprising that they should treat
us with suspicion at first. There was a special reason for this, as
I soon learnt. My own arrival coincided with that of a message
saying that ninety Viet-Namese soldiers had come across the
frontier and were occupying a village on the Cambodian side.
The messenger was a tribesman, so his story had to be translated for the Cambodian Governor, in whose office we were now
sitting. A Cambodian partisan had been wounded, the messenger
said, and was being brought to Bokeo. The day on which the
incident had taken place was the day we had left Viet-Nam and
crossed the border. I remembered the single shot we heard in
the afternoon. After a look at the map, it seemed that my party
must have been a long way from the scene of the action. 'Ninety'
men sounded ominously like the section of sixty said by the Viet-
Namese to have been absent from camp for a week already. After
my journey I read reports of frontier incidents elsewhere along the
sugar-palm curtain. I daresay the Cambodians and Viet-Namese
were equally to blame. These incidents continued in 1958, and
the one I witnessed was not an isolated event. However, I was
prompted to ask why these two friendly countries were involved
in this hit-and-run warfare. The Cambodians confirmed that it
was they who had blocked the old road number nineteen. The
felling of trees had been a unilateral measure to stop pilfering.
The Viet-Namese side of the border was said to be open. The

Cambodians were at a disadvantage because some forty kilometres separated their post from the actual frontier. Their ideas about the Viet-Namese frontier-post were vague. They knew it was nearer the border than their own post. The distance would not have mattered if they had had jeeps to use on the few motorable tracks. But they had none.

'We used to have proper vehicles,' they said, 'till the Americans withdrew them.' At this time the U.S.A. was delivering, and withdrawing, military equipment to and from Cambodia and South Viet-Nam. It did not seem to make sense.

The problem of my arrival took second place while Cambodians ran backward and forward sending messages and organizing counter-patrols. When the Governor had had time to read my letter of introduction, he sent a radio-message to the Provincial Governor of Stung-Treng and received permission to grant me facilities. This was all according to plan, for I had made the necessary arrangements with the Cambodian Ministry of Interior at an earlier date. We settled down again with the map, and tried to discover more about the Viet-Namese raid. The messenger was bad at answering questions. Later in the day another message came that thirty Viet-Namese commanded by an officer were moving towards Bokeo. A Cambodian patrol prepared to leave at once. It was a good opportunity for me to go with them. But six days was too long to spend on a jaunt, which, as the soldiers said gaily, would lead only to the scene of the crime. There would be no hope of catching the raiders red-handed. The soldiers who did these patrols were not tribesmen but uncompromising Cambodians, men to whom Stung-Treng province was a wild and inhospitable place. Some of them regarded it as a punishment to be posted there, as a Cockney National Serviceman might regard Catterick or Bodmin. I knew the homes of these young soldiers very well. They came from the rich rice-growing plains in the south. For a year or two they had to forget their native villages, forget the slender betel-palms, smiling lotus-pools, and stately monasteries. I shared their nostalgia, and take this opportunity of warning the reader that this journey through Cambodia did not traverse the most typical regions.

The frontier Governor – equivalent to a District Officer – had served twenty-five years with the French. Beyond retiring age, he was under special contract with the Cambodian Government, who, in the first years of independence, were perpetually short of experienced men. A genial soul from a rich province in central Cambodia, he complained that life on the frontier was far too rough. There was, for example, nothing to eat. Notwithstanding this remark, he commanded a cuisine which would have made the mouth water in any country. There was venison chopped and tender, onion and herbs mixed with meat and wrapped in lettuce, all dipped in a piquant sauce. To follow, there was Indian curry and a whole roast chicken. After my rice and salt diet, this good food was an unexpected luxury. Wild animals were kept as pets – a magnificent mountain goat which came when you called it by name, and a small black honey-bear. The goat was mascot of the Army. The bear belonged to the Governor. 'I don't know its sex,' he said. 'But I feed it on wild honey.'

The presence of Chinese restaurateurs at Bokeo was a sign that this frontier station was in touch with the outside world. Cambodia has a Chinese minority, more than 300,000 strong, which has been arriving from China on and off since the days of Angkor. One Chinese visitor to Angkor in the thirteenth century wrote:

'The palace-staff alone may wear cloth with two types of embroidered flowers. Among the people, only the women are allowed to do this. A Chinaman, who recently arrived, wore material embroidered with two types of flowers; but he was not prosecuted as he did not know about the customs.'

Even today the Chinese do not always observe Cambodian customs. I have seen them abstain from taking off their hats within the precinct of a Buddhist monastery, and when they enter the temple itself refuse to remove their shoes. These are the two rudest things which you can do in Buddhist Cambodia. I once saw an old Cambodian woman watch a French settler do exactly the same thing. 'That's where he'll go,' she said, and pointed to a picture of Buddhist Hell. Though Cambodians complained more about the politics than the customs of their Chinese minority, they depended on them for the internal and external trade of the country, including the café business. In this remote frontier-post, bowls of steaming noodles were being served by pale-faced Chinese cooks.

On the opposite hillside Buddhist monks were hanging out their saffron robes in the morning sun. In the days of Angkor the Cambodians alternated between being Hindu Sivaites and Buddhists of the Northern School. In the fourteenth century, a new type of Buddhism, the Southern School, spread to Cambodia from Ceylon. This is the Buddhism practised by Cambodia's 41 millions today. About 80,000 of them are Buddhist monks, wearing the yellow robe of Buddha. This Southern School Buddhism, which is practised in Burma, Ceylon, Thailand, and Laos, as well as in Cambodia, is also known as 'Little Vehicle', 'Hinayana', or 'Theravada' (Teaching of the Elders). At Bokeo there was no Buddhist monastery properly speaking, only a *Sala Tien*, that is a place where alms can be offered to Buddhist monks. This alms-house had been in existence for sixteen years. All the monks were Laotian except the head monk, a Cambodian from the south-west. The reason for this was that Stung-Treng province lies on Cambodia's frontier with Laos, as well as with Viet-Nam. There is a considerable Laotian minority living within Cambodia. When I made my visit to the almshouse four or five monks were present, and about the same number of novices. Two monks were temporarily absent. They had gone more than twenty miles to say Buddhist prayers in the house of a dead farmer. They had left on foot and were not expected to return till the next day.

I asked the Head Monk whether the tribesmen paid any attention to Buddhism. They passed the monastery every day, he said, but rarely came inside. If they did venture in, the monks gave them instruction on how to bow down before statues of Buddha or the Buddhist clergy. At festival times the tribesmen would join the crowd to see what went on. The 2,500th anniversary of the Buddhist Era had been celebrated earlier the same year. Cambodians at Bokeo had nearly all accepted the Ten Buddhist Precepts, donning the traditional white garments. Shadowy angel-like figures could have been seen flitting among the trees of the forest. Twenty-five citizens had taken the yellow robe of Buddhist monk. Among them had been the officer commanding, a young Lieutenant. Educated at a Roman Catholic school in Phnom Penh, the capital, he had never become a monk previously. His comment on a week's experience was: 'I found the life of Buddhist prayer extremely tough.' I questioned him about his Roman Catholic education. He said that his case was no different from that of his fellow-students. They paid lip-service to the beliefs of their teachers, and went through the motions of any form of worship on which the missionaries insisted, but as soon as they left school premises they reverted to their traditional Buddhist beliefs.

At the previous full moon another big Buddhist festival had been celebrated. Outside my room in the military encampment there was a wooden box full of cardboard masks coated with silver and coloured paper. The masks had been specially made for a theatre show organized by the soldiers to raise money for the Buddhist monks. This kind of popular theatre exists all over Cambodia. The masks were recognizable copies of those worn by the Royal Cambodian Ballet in the capital, Phnom Penh. I asked one of the soldiers which play had been performed, hoping he might answer 'Ream Ker', Cambodia's epic poem. This is the same poem as the Indian epic, the *Ramayana,* from which the Royal Cambodian Ballet chooses much of its finest repertoire. The interesting thing is that the *Ream Ker* has characters and episodes which do not occur in the Indian version. Unfortunately, most of the Cambodian version is still missing. Till quite recently Cambodian farmers would borrow ancient manuscripts from monastery collections, read them under the shade of a betel-palm, letting the pages blow away across the ricefields when they dropped off to sleep. I have visited many Cambodian monasteries in the hope of finding some of the missing chapters, but so far without success. Anyway, the soldiers had not been performing the *Ream Ker,* but another favourite *Sre Krup Leak (The Woman with all the Virtues).* I asked one of the soldiers about it, but though he had seen it many times, he could not tell me the plot. It was pleasing to find these peasant-soldiers of South Cambodia bringing their traditional theatre to the forests of this distant frontier region.

'Did the Pnong come to watch?' I asked.

Pnong is the generic word used in Cambodia to denote the tribes, whether or not the tribes referred to are in fact 'Pnong'. For there is a Pnong tribe, which I encountered later.

'Yes, they came to watch,' said the soldier.

'Did they laugh?' I asked.

'Yes,' he said, 'they laughed and laughed. Some of them laughed so much that they cried. I saw tears running down their cheeks myself.'

These tribes have felt the partial imprint of Khmer civilization for many centuries, so it is natural they enjoy watching a Cambodian theatre-show. It was now possible to begin a comparison between the 'Viet-Namization' of tribesmen in Viet-Nam and 'Cambodianization' of tribesmen in this northeastern province of Cambodia. At Pim's village I had heard the children sing songs in praise of the Viet-Namese President. Here, in Cambodia, there were none – that is I heard none – singing in praise of the Cambodian king. Not yet. The Cambodians were contending with the difficulty that the non-tribal population of this province is mostly Laotian. So besides teaching Cambodian to the tribesmen, the Cambodians were having to teach it to the Laotians as well.

The tribal villages were grouped in cantons. The Governor had decided that forty-five hamlets were too many for one canton. I witnessed a meeting at which he split the one canton into four. It was all done in a fatherly, democratic way, which brought credit on the Cambodian governor. Village headmen were summoned into the office. There were one or two absentees, not surprising when one considered that communications in the jungle only existed by runner.

Representatives of the first ten villages were put in a group and told to elect a leader. The leader's village was to be the administrative centre of a new canton. They smoked their tribal pipes, talking hard and sometimes glancing at the Cambodian Governor, who spoke through an interpreter much as the French used to do in their day. When a decision was reached, hands were raised. On a given signal, they clapped in unison.

'What's your name?' the winner was asked.

'Bat Deng,' he said.

'Age?'

'Age?' he replied. 'I don't know. We tribesmen don't know about age.'

Sometimes I met Cambodians who said the same kind of thing. 'We countryfolk don't know about hours, or kilometres, or anything like that.'

The Governor was too advanced in years to go into the tribal villages himself. He had tried doing so, but found the going too rough and the ceremonial jars of honour too indigestible. The deficiency was made good by the Cambodian Lieutenant, young and very active. This frontier-post was lucky to have two efficient leaders working closely together.

CHAPTER THIRTEEN

DIGGING FOR ZIRCONS

This frontier-post of Bokeo was famous for one reason – its precious stones, zircons. The word 'zircon', derived from Arabic, is used generically to describe certain silicates, hyacinth for example, which can be cut and used as gems. These Cambodian zircons are called diamonds by enthusiasts, The surrounding hillsides were honeycombed with deserted zircon-pits – like disused wells. During the war Viet-Minh Communists who operated round here were afraid of falling down pits and breaking their necks in the dark. Some of the holes were very overgrown. Up and down the bamboo-clad hillsides, hundreds of diggers staked claims daily as they dug for zircons. Work did not begin in earnest till ten in the morning. Trees shaded the pits, and digging continued through midday up till four in the afternoon. The pits then in use lay a kilometre behind the Buddhist monastery. Pnong, Laotian, Cambodian, Burmese, and Viet-Namese miners were digging and sifting, or digging and washing. I was surprised to find Chinese, also, doing this manual work. I asked them in Cantonese what race they were. 'Hakkas' they replied – the nomads of South China. Some of the Pnong looked like Red Indians with their long black hair and red skin. Of course, their skins were not naturally red. The earth round Bokeo is *terre rouge*.

The pits were measured in 'hat'. The 'hat' is a Cambodian measure, from the tip of the middle finger to the elbow, roughly equivalent to nineteen inches. The pits at the bottom of the hill were shallow – eight or nine 'hat'. Higher up there were holes twenty or thirty 'hat' deep. The diameter of a pit would be two or three 'hat'. Steps were gouged out of the walls, permitting the diggers to descend one at a time into the earth. Some pits had subterranean tunnels and half-finished underground chambers. Earlier in the week there had been an earth-fall, burying one of the miners for more than an hour. The rescuers had been forced to uncover a large area before getting him out alive.

I stripped to the waist and climbed down one of the smaller pits. At the bottom I found that the digger had been undermining one of the walls in his search for jewels. I was afraid the pit-edge would cave in when loafers crowded to the edge of the hole to see what the foreigner was doing. Their faces peered flatly from a circular piece of blue sky, which diminished in size as I went down and down. The circular pattern of their heads was framed against brightness, their expressions Jerome Boschlike as they peered downwards. I brought up a basketful of earth from the pit and sorted it myself by hand. Several times I thought I had found a zircon. After scraping off mud, it was always a stone. Then I found something knobbly. As I scraped off the earth, there, sure enough, was the reddish tint which I had learnt to recognize from other people's treasure. This tint was a deposit left by zircons – which had already been removed. The diggers said I could hardly, even with beginner's luck, expect to find anything in such a small amount of earth.

Though hundreds of diggers were at work in scores of pits, it would be misleading to say the place was a hive of activity. There are no hives of activity at all in Cambodia. That is the charm of the country. Work in the zircon-pits takes place at the digger's own Cambodian speed in his own Cambodian time. It took several days to dig a pit. The earth was heaped up and covered

Digging for zircons at Bokeo

with bamboo till the digger had time to sort it. The women would sift earth through their fingers, squeezing anything that looked like a zircon. The earth could also be sieved by a professional siever who worked at a muddy pool. Cambodians were specializing in this work. Their sharp eyes soon picked out jewels from the slushy mess of gravel and mud. Each pit-owner had a piece of hollow bamboo in which he stored the day's treasure, but some people hunted all day without finding anything. Most of the uncut zircon lumps were sold to Chinese and Burmese dealers on the spot. They fetched four hundred riels each. Large pieces were rare, and fetched eight hundred. A zircon the size of my lump with the red deposit could have been sold for five thousand if it had really been a jewel. The riel, derived no doubt from the Portuguese *real,* is the unit of Cambodian currency.

Though failing in my search for zircons, I had better luck with Neolithic tools. The Laotian word for 'thunder axe' is 'kwong knock-a-bar', at least that's what it sounds like. I approached some villagers who said they had seen these stones in the forest beside streams, but had none in their houses. Then I was directed to the home of two old Burmese. 'Yes,' they said, 'we have some "kwong knock-a-bar".' The amount of old junk which they kept as medicine was amazing. Now it was all put out on view – roots, fruit, animal skin, old leather, pebbles, and bottles. In all these rags and bones there was not one 'kwong knock-a-bar'. When they had failed, I was sent to a big house outside the camp. It belonged to Mr R.K.

R.K. was a little old Laotian who spoke no Cambodian. When he heard what I wanted, he fetched a sack from his bedroom. It was full of tiny stone axe-heads with smooth handles. I laid them out while R.K. polished the prize piece, which looked like a bronze axe-head. Its handle was rather short. R.K. explained that a piece had been cut off to make a bracelet for the previous Governor's wife. The bronze implement, if indeed it was an ancient tool, was hollow and open at the handle end where it had been cut. The anvil was stained with a blue and white chalk-like substance. It looked as if R.K. had been using it as a pestle for mixing medicinal pastes. I explained that I wanted some 'kwong knock-a-bar' to take to England, and was wondering how best to strike a bargain for the stone tools. Money resources were low till I could reach Stung-Treng, whither I had sent a money-order. After a moment's hesitation, R.K. divided his collection in half and poured a little heap of axe-heads into my open hands.

He gathered up the others into his sack and took them back to the bedroom at once. I never saw the bronze object again. It was R.K.'s dearest possession, and I doubted if he would ever part with it. I stuffed the axe-heads into my pocket, so that the gathering loafers did not know we had conducted any business at all.

R.K. had not finished. He brought out a bottle of viscous yellow fluid. It was medicine of his own concoction based on a recipe handed down from his grandparents. It was effective, he said, when all European medicines failed. He told me it was intended for my long journey to England, when I would surely need potent drugs to ward off evil spirits and sickness. I had not the heart to tell R.K. that my rucksack weighed too much already without taking on bottles of viscous tonic which I might never wish to use. I had accepted the axe-heads, and I could hardly refuse the medicine. Perhaps it would be useful in villages where they were always asking for cures. I asked R.K. the size of a normal dose.

'This medicine,' he replied, 'is made from seven different kinds of jungle produce. It cannot be taken orally. If you drink it, you will die. It makes the body go all — '. Here I could not understand the Cambodian word used by my interpreter. It might have been 'faint' or 'paralysed', according to the way he was clutching at his throat. 'It has to be injected,' continued R.K. He proudly unwrapped an oblong package. Inside there was a shiny syringe and a wicked-looking needle which he, fitted up so quickly I was afraid he would demonstrate its powers on one of us. I had no hypodermic myself, nor I felt sure had the tribal villages through which we would be passing. I dared not give the tonic to tribesmen who would certainly take it orally, perhaps with resultant paralysis and sudden death. We parked the bottle next to some rice where it would not break, though secretly I hoped it would.

The Lieutenant gave me an idea of the tribes and wild animals we could expect to meet on the way. Tigers were common. There were also panther, and allegedly a very occasional rhinoceros. There were plenty of wild elephants. We had seen their tracks already. They could be tracked to hills, where they liked to lie up during the daytime. The tribesmen sometimes held elephant hunts, after which the captured beasts would be tamed and used as means of transport. The Lieutenant said he preferred to walk. It was more comfortable. News on the tiger-front was that the region was full of them. A new incident was reported at a village three kilometres away. Two buffalo-sized tigers had taken a dog for their breakfast. Villagers had seen the brutes and given ineffective chase.

I was next told about the many different tribes in North-East Cambodia. To the north, the Cavet, Cachak, and Kiting, of whom I had never heard. In the direction I would now be taking, there lived the Tompuon (see Fig. 1, p. 33). It was difficult to distinguish between the many different tribes, for you would find dissimilar physical types in the same village. At first sight the Tompuon seemed smaller, but later we met tall ones as well. They cut off tips of their teeth in the middle of the mouth – a useful mark of recognition. By now I knew the Jerai tribesmen well, from their long black hair, often fixed with a slide at the back. The mop of hair made the boys look as if they had stepped out of an early Italian painting. From the neck upwards they might have been labelled 'School of Raphael'.

My stay at this Cambodian frontier-post had been so pleasant that I was reluctant to leave. The next port-of-call would be Stung-Treng. We left camp a party of three, myself and two Cambodian soldiers. The tribesmen provided relays of guides. In theory we could walk forty kilometres in a day and reach a large village by the evening. In fact, we spent the night at a Tompuon tribal village on the way. The going was not difficult. First, a good earth track, then a jungle path. Sometimes we had to make detours round fallen trees, and seemed to be losing height. We were approaching a big tributary of the River Mekong. We had turned south-west to reach it, as I could see from the different way in which our shadows splayed out across the path. At times we seemed to be walking almost due south. My two Cambodian soldiers were products of the home counties, if one may coin this expression for the rice-growing provinces round Cambodia's capital, Phnom Penh. They proved excellent companions. Like true Cambodians, they complained about the distance, and let the tribesmen carry their military rucksacks. Time passed quickly listening to their amiable chatter and badinage. Above our heads jungle-birds flew back and forth – blue, golden and red. The blue birds flamed brighter than the tropical sky above. There are countless shades of green in the Cambodian forest, but none which specially sticks in my mind. Not being a naturalist, I need some human association before a feature of the landscape takes root in my consciousness. For example, when walking in the forest, I long to see the sprawling fronds of a banana-tree because I know that this is often a sign of human habitation.

At three o'clock we reached an overgrown tribal village five hours short of the river. There would be no more villages after this, not a house, not even a ricefield till we reached the river itself. I had developed tummy trouble, and suddenly felt very ill. It was the kind of illness one ought to expect, and I had been lucky not to have it before. In less than an hour I seemed to lose all my strength. It was an absurd effort of will-power to stagger out into the forest, where one dug little holes and filled them like a cat. Pigs followed, waiting to dig up and eat what had been so carefully buried. When I refused food, the soldiers looked anxious and assumed in their private chit-chat that I had been a stretcher case all the way from Viet-Nam. They discussed endlessly whether I would be fit to walk the five hours to the river in the morning. The only food I felt like taking was a plate of jungle potatoes. One of the tribesmen kindly boiled them specially for me.

Night came, but I could not sleep. Outside, the Tompuon tribesmen were holding a festival. I wiped away sweat from my face with a dirty handkerchief, and raised myself on an elbow. I could hear women singing little airs – a few bars only, then they would stop and laugh, letting someone else have a go. One of them strummed a stringed instrument. There was another noise easy to recognize – the regular plash of water as a jar was refilled. Shades of Pim's village! It was just over three weeks since I set off from the Copper Tower at Binh-Dinh. I must have covered rather more than two hundred miles.

Note

The stone tools mentioned in this chapter have been examined by Mr. G. de G. Sieveking of the British Museum. Mr. Sieveking, who has carried out prehistoric excavations in South-East Asia, tells me that these 'shouldered adzes' as they are known can be dated approximately to 500–700 B.C.

CHAPTER FOURTEEN

HALF-WAY TO ANGKOR

In the morning I was well enough to continue our journey, but did not yet feel like eating. We set off at seven with tribal guides, who agreed to go with us the whole way to the river. After an hour there was a biggish stream of which the map made no mention. Tribesmen had felled a tree, which made crossing easy. The next landmark was a cart-track. Traces of an ox-cart could be seen distinctly in the mud. This was another sign that we had come off the plateau and were descending into the great Cambodian plain. The tribes behind us did not have carts. Cambodians have carts, the same kind of carts which they used in the time of Angkor. The kind of cart which they used then can be seen sculptured on the walls of Khmer monuments at Angkor and elsewhere. It was exciting to enter the 'cart' country. From now on there would be cart-tracks all the way to Angkor. Some of them would actually follow traces of the ancient Khmer road from Prah Khan to Angkor, but I had yet to find any traces of an ancient road this side of Prah Khan.

We came out of the forest on to a broad plain shimmering with rice. It was not quite ripe. Walking, we had outstripped the season of harvest. Then, for the first time on the journey, we saw the sight which is so familiar in Cambodia – Buddhist monks washing their saffron robes in the waters of a lazy river. This was the Sre Pak river which brings the rains of the plateau down to the River Mekong. After days of dirty jungle-pools and streams, it was heart-warming to see a river. Beside the Buddhist monastery, there was a village. My two Cambodian soldiers doffed their bush-hats as we passed the entrance to the monastery, then they led me to a small military camp beside the river. The sergeant in command of this camp had been warned by radio that I was coming. This remote riverside camp was a happy place thanks to the enlightened policy of the Cambodian Government in allowing wives and families to accompany husbands. The wives especially were in excellent spirits, judging from the remarks I heard floating out of kitchen windows.

There was no difficulty in making contact with these Cambodians, for I knew their language. They held a kind of non-stop press conference round my bedside. Everyone wished to have a word with the foreigner in his little bamboo hut. Some wanted medicine. Others asked questions about England. One of them watched me writing my diary, asked the usual questions, then said that in Cambodian there was a word to describe people like me. I asked what word.

'*Pryke*,' he replied.

I had always, rightly or wrongly, used the word *pryke* to translate the English word 'wise'. 'No,' I protested. 'Only old people are wise.' He tried speaking in French, and was even wider the mark with *philosophe*. This educated attempt to assess me was rather unusual. The average Cambodian peasant would simply tell his friends that I was a 'map-man' because he had noted that I was the owner of a map.

The next morning I saw some soldiers playing with two chestnut ponies in the camp compound. It started with a successful attempt to make the animals stand on their hindlegs like circus-performers. Two soldiers then began belabouring one of the ponies with heavy wooden poles. The poor beast frisked up and down as the sharp blows fell repeatedly on its nose and legs.

The other soldiers thought this was so funny that they picked up logs of smouldering wood from the previous night's camp-fire, and hurled them in the pony's face. The womenfolk stopped their work and enjoyed the spectacle as much as the men. It was hard to match this cruelty to animals with the tolerance which is the average Cambodian's most delightful quality.

Later the same morning I saw the Buddhist monks file out from the monastery and line up on the path with their backs to the river. Each monk carried a large globular begging-bowl. Half turned left, and half right. Then they marched off in two Indian files on the daily begging-quest for food. Cambodians believe that the giving of food to Buddhist monks is one of the most effective ways of acquiring Buddhist merit. The monks eat twice a day – rice soup about seven-thirty in the morning, and one big meal of rice before midday. In forest regions they live on rice alone, since the villagers have few vegetables to offer them. The monks have to season their rice with a piquant paste made from crushed mint leaves and salt, or else a strong-smelling salty fish paste called prahoc. This makes a poor diet, but since the monks are accustomed to it since childhood, they do not seem to mind. Some of the older monks eat once only, about eleven, and miss out the seven-thirty meal.

The rice had not yet been harvested in this village, and the farmers were gloomy about its prospects. Earlier in the season the river had risen like a tidal wave and flooded the ricefields just when the grain was beginning to ripen. The flood-water had gone down quickly, but the river's few hours' spate had ruined much of the harvest. I asked them how they would manage without rice. 'We don't know,' they said. 'But it's happened before, and we just live on what there is till the next harvest.' A Chinese description of thirteenth-century Angkor says there were three or four rice-harvests a year, yet in modern Cambodia there are, in most regions, only one or two. Ancient inscriptions tell us that tens and hundreds of thousands of men were employed on building temples such as Angkor Wat, but they do not explain the relation between ancient Khmer buildings and the water-drainage system which seemed an integral part of their town-planning. Which was more important – the building of canals for irrigation or the building of a temple for a god? An answer to this question will answer that old conundrum of French scholars 'Why did the ancient Khmer empire collapse?' Was it because they built too many temples and wore themselves out, or did something go wrong with the irrigation system? Ancient Khmer inscriptions praise their king, 'who by raising a holy barrage has made the water to flow where before there was little or none ... a reservoir, beautiful as the moon, to refresh mankind'. The ancient Khmers were obsessed with water. The artificial reservoirs at Angkor had a capacity of more than 60 million cubic metres each. Was all this water for economic or religious purposes? For both, of course, but which came first – a temple for a deified king, or ricefields for the Khmer people? Anyway, the irrigation system fell into disrepair, so that today Cambodian farmers are for the most part left to the mercy of drought and flood.

Illness left me weak, so I took a needed rest at this riverside village. When I felt well enough, I walked lazily through the ricefields up to the fringes of the jungle. Flights of birds wheeled overhead. As I lay in the long grass, a bird swooped down on to the branches of a nearby tree, where his breast-feathers matched the leaves turning golden in the evening sun. I was now half-way from the coast to Angkor with about two hundred and twenty miles left to do, but so far I had found no traces of the ancient Khmer road. There was little I could do but keep a watchful eye open and ask questions in all the villages. I estimated that it would take me another six or seven days to reach the River Mekong at Stung-Treng. For the next few days I would be among Laotians. Many of them live along the River Sre Pok, whose banks I now followed all the way to the Mekong.

CHAPTER FIFTEEN

LAOTIAN VILLAGES

The new guides were Laotian, one of them so black he looked like an African. There were scars on his upper arm where a tiger had clawed him outside the village. After thirty-minutes' walk we found fresh tiger paw-marks on the sandy path – very large paw-marks, I thought. No doubt, a very large tiger. There was high grass and scrub fringing the path. A large animal scuffled away under our noses, or so it seemed.

'Tiger?' I wondered.

'Only a wild pig,' said the guides.

After seeing the dead tiger at Cuty, I had no desire to meet a live one, but had a presentiment that if we did meet one it would be on a day when I did not have a colour film in the camera. Today's film was black and white. Three hours' walk brought us to a village where the guides had to be changed. A giant snake had been caught in the marsh. Its skin was stretched out on a pole to dry. Standing up on end it was almost as tall as the house. The skin would be treated in a special way to preserve it, and then sold in the market at Stung-Treng for whatever the Chinese merchants would pay.

The villages here took their names from the river, Sre Pok, adding a 'little' or 'big'. Little Sre Pok could have been a prosperous riverside village, but it was so far from a road that there was no way of selling its produce. There were no resident merchants either. The villagers had little incentive for growing fruit or vegetables, though the river-banks were potentially just

Its skin was stretched out on a pole to dry

as rich as those which bordered the River Mekong in South and
Central Cambodia. Moreover, the rice harvested was insufficient
for a year's food supply. Until the new crop, the people had to
live on a starvation diet of fruit, roots, and whatever came to
hand. Several times a year they harnessed their bullock-carts and
made the long journey to Stung-Treng. They were afraid to go
singly, and travelled in caravans of three or four carts together. At
nightfall they would unharness the oxen and sleep in the forest.

Chinese merchants in the market at Stung-Treng paid ridicu-lously low prices for the country produce. The peasants accepted these prices, bought salt, and returned home uncomplaining.

At Big Srepok the people claimed their village had never been visited by a European before. I doubted the truth of this. They had some odd things to say. Was it true, for example, that there were two kinds of Europeans, those with black eyes and those with white? Were all European countries divided in two according to the colour of the inhabitants' eyes? When they heard I was English, and not French, they peered into my face and said knowingly that Frenchmen's eyes were different. They looked at the Neolithic axe-heads which I had collected earlier on the journey. According to their local legend, these stones are fabricated by the Chinese regularly each year. They are then offered to various Chinese gods, who scatter them over the earth during thunderstorms. Although Laotian, they were bilingual and some of them spoke Cambodian well. According to tradi-tion, Sre Pok meant Lady Pok, a warrior queen, who came out of Laos many years ago and colonized the banks of the river, which was thereafter named in her honour. Some of their finest houses were built without nails. Solid wooden bolts had been used instead. I remembered the tribal schoolmaster at Cuty, who said improvements could not be made in his school buildings because the Government provided no money for buying nails.

The next two and half days had much the same pattern, long walks through the open forest and grassy savannah. Up above, a burning blue sky. Sometimes a cool wind blew across the plain. It was November – the beginning of Cambodia's two-month cold season. The wind brought coughs and sore throats to the villages. The peasants would go to bed in the evening feeling warm, but caught cold before dawn, when the temperature fell to its lowest. As the days passed, my legs grew stronger again. Old blisters disappeared. New ones came. Nothing could diminish the exhilaration of striding through the forest, ever westwards, nearer each day to the fabulous ruins of Angkor the Great.

Villages occurred more or less as I had them marked on the map, though one had been abandoned. Many of the peasants had two houses, a largish house on the fringe of their ancestral rice-fields, where they would spend seven or eight months of the year, and another smaller but in the riverside village near a Buddhist almshouse or monastery. When working in the ricefields, they would send special food to the monastery for the Buddhist monks. The houses of village headmen were scattered to all four corners of the savannah. One evening we marched to the edge of the rice-plain, and were told the headman had left his ricefield house for a 'remote region' on a fishing trip. When this happened, we just sat down and waited for his return, though it was usually possible to find one of the assistant headmen. Their harvest varied from fair to bad. There had been too little rain, afterwards too much. Some farmers had lost a fifth, others nearly a whole year's crop. The streams, from which drinking-water was drawn, were almost dry already, though the rainy season had only just finished. The muddy stream-water tasted delicious after a long walk. Water from the Sre Pok river had a rancid flavour. The Sre Pok rapids were often within earshot of the track, but it was a bad season for taking boats down them. The villagers were willing to try, if I had wished to go by water. There were two main paths leading west. One went from village to village, which was the path we always took. Another passed north of the ricefields and houses, linking the villages more directly with the western regions.

One of the Laotian guides had an enormous black moustache. The other was a burly man from Central Laos. He spoke good

Cambodian and confided to me that Stung-Treng province really belonged to Laos and not Cambodia. One day we were sitting by a lake in the middle of the forest. I was watching out for big game when one of the guides said:

'Is Cambodia at war?'

'No,' I said, 'Cambodia is not at war, as far as I know.' 'They're not at war with Viet-Nam, are they?' he pressed me to reply again.

'No,' I said. 'I don't think so.'

'Then can you tell us,' they both asked together, 'why all the young men and women are being trained to use rifles?'

Later on I was asked these questions again and again. Whatever soft-soap answers I gave, they were convinced that fighting would break out any minute. One day I entered a village where training was in progress. There were a dozen young men and women sloping arms with imitation guns made of wood. The Headman smiled as he saw me watching this curious and rather efficient-looking display.

'What's it all about?' he asked. 'The bachelors have been conscripted, also all the unmarried women.'

The headman's fifteen-year-old daughter, a fine-looking Cambodian girl, was among the trainees. Later in the morning she came back from the forest parade-ground looking very hot. Without saying a word, she returned to her daily work of pounding rice. I pitied the instructor most of all. He had to tramp from village to village, being criticized by all and sundry for omitting this or that hamlet from his programme. They also blamed him for making hours of training longer at one village than at another. 'This is not some nonentity's idea,' he announced to his trainees. 'It comes straight from the King. Our national hero, Prince Norodom Sihanouk, wishes us to get ourselves into training.' After this oration, he turned and saw me. In order, I think, to impress his audience, he ordered a search of my luggage. We opened up the rucksack, and I hurled its contents all round the forest glade. The people were so ashamed to see these innocent objects of apparel inspected that afterwards I was treated with extra-special politeness and respect. One of the guides called me 'Venerable', the phrase reserved for a layman addressing a Buddhist monk or an unimportant Cambodian speaking to a Cabinet Minister. 'Venerable' is an inadequate translation, for it adds the idea of 'old age' which is sometimes absent in the original. In my case I was about half the age of the gentleman who was calling me 'Venerable'.

CHAPTER SIXTEEN

REACHING THE MEKONG

For several days we had been passing through Laotian villages, then suddenly we were in among the Pnong.

'Are you really Pnong?' I asked them. 'And not some other tribe?'

'Yes,' they said, we are the real Pnong.'

'Are you sure you're not Jerai?' I asked.

'Jerai?' they answered, and it was clear from the look on their faces that the tribe I had so lately visited was a complete mystery to this other tribe – the Pnong. Like the Jerai and Bahnars, the 'Pnong drink rice-alcohol at festivals. Their hair is tied at the back in buns, and they wear enormous chunks of ivory, or wood, in their ears. Sometimes they remove these ornaments, exposing a gaping hole in a much-stretched ear-lobe. While we rested in the shade of some huts a banana-tree crashed down at our feet just missing the baggage. There were other signs of neglect besides overgrown banana-trees. The Pnongs wanted medicine. The most pathetic request came from a very old woman who asked for strength pills and then for ointment to stop her eyes growing dim with age.

There were no two opinions about the military training. It was disliked. Fathers and grandfathers of the Pnong, they said, had never been forced to learn arms drill by anyone. They regarded themselves as a peace-loving people who wished nothing more than to cultivate their ricefields in peace. Oh, for the days of the French,' I heard one extremist say. He complained that his monthly wages had not been paid by the Cambodians, who told him 'the money has run out'. I was not able to check up on his story, but it illustrated what sometimes happened in post-independence Cambodia, where foreign aid brought in three times as much cash as the Cambodian national income. When money ran out, that was that until the next quarter's aid came through.

News of my arrival crept round the village. One by one, the Pnong came to the bamboo shelter where we were sitting, and went through the motions of what was to me a well-defined ritual. First, obeisance, three times on hands and knees, as if I were a Buddhist monk. Then each suppliant gave me a bowl of rice, sticks of incense, and one or two hen's eggs. They seemed to think that offering me food was an act which would earn them Buddhist merit. All had been copied from Cambodian Buddhist practices, though eggs are not normally offered as alms. The reaction of these Pnong to my presence was a new experience, different from that of their half-brothers at Pim's village. Did they think I was some kind of holy man? I had often heard Buddhist monks repeat set formulae when receiving offerings of food. I knew one of these by heart, and repeated it to the Pnong. 'Sathu' they echoed reverently. Sathu is a kind of Buddhist Amen. It was like taking part in the Buddhist equivalent of a Black Mass, but gave me some evidence that the tribesmen of this region are deeply influenced by Cambodian ways. The same could not be said of the tribesmen I had seen in Viet-Nam, who rather disliked Viet-Namese ways. As far as I could judge from this single journey through the tribal areas of Viet-Nam and Cambodia, I would say that the tribesmen like 'Cambodianization', or 'Khmerizing' as it is called, better than being turned into chopstick-using Viet-Namese. The reason may be that the Cambodians and tribesmen have a common origin, whereas the Viet-Namese are outsiders who came from the direction of China long ago and took by force the coastal plain which they occupy today.

The eggs, given to me by the Pnong, made a variation on my perpetual diet of rice and salt. Some villagers served sticky rice with a delicious straight-from-the-field taste. At other times the rice was grey-brown and tasteless. I developed a liking for the charred crust of rice from the bottom of the pot. When rice is freshly cooked, and served hot, it is very palatable, even without anything to go with it. The crossbow from Pim's village was an object of admiration among the Pnong. It interested them more than either my camera or my wristwatch. They had never seen anything like my Jerai sabre, either. 'Clean' was the adjective of praise which they used to describe it. They wanted to buy it, but had no money. The story of my journey was repeated over and over again, how I had been given the crossbow to take to my home village, but how I had bought the sabre to defend myself from tigers. We conversed in Cambodian.

The next day we crossed and recrossed the Sre Pok river in deep-scraped canoes made by the Pnong from tree-trunks. Then we walked a long way through the forest. The guides were too lazy to walk, so an ox-cart was prepared. I was glad to let the cart carry my rucksack. The track was so bumpy that I feared something would break when the luggage bounced about. Before I could do anything about it, a bag of photographic equipment crashed on to the path, but luckily nothing was broken. On the twenty-eighth day of the journey we came to an ancient monument, not alas an ancient Khmer monument, but the ruins of a French colonial bridge. This bridge, which once carried vehicles across the Sre Pok river, lay blown to bits by the Viet-Minh Communists. Its ruins were forlorn. There was a sandy beach round its twisted girders, where soldiers washed laundry or went for a swim. A precipitous path led to a ferry. The ferrymen were leading ideal Cambodian lives. Days passed without any vehicles coming in sight. A Cambodian police-post guarded the ferry. It must have been one of the remotest postings in the country. At night the barbed-wire gate dosed, but there were too few policemen to mount a guard. All was silent till dawn.

The police gave me a royal reception, which included a fresh pineapple, the first I had tasted on this journey. The medical store-keeper turned out to be a cultured young Cambodian, other members of whose family were studying in Europe. His long slit eyes did not seem to match his dark skin. Sure enough, he came from a mixture of Chinese and Cambodian parentage with a grandmother who was pure Chinese. The next day, he accompanied me on my journey. We started before dawn in the hope of seeing big game, but had no luck. There was a village three hours walk from the broken bridge. It lay just off the track, beside a hill. There was delay finding guides, and it was after midday when we set off into the forest once more. The two guides, prematurely old-looking men, walked at a rattling pace. Down dale, over ridges, in and out of jungle, and across the dried-up beds of streams we went. An hour after dark they said they had lost the way. We had to make do with light from the waxing moon of a new month. It lay just above the tree-tops in the direction we were heading. Then clouds covered it, and we could no longer see the path beneath our feet. The sand was deep, and there were narrow ruts made by generations of ox-carts, which made it difficult to balance because of the top-heavy rucksack. Once or twice I fell down. The guides looked at each other in alarmed silence.

After six and half hours' walk the guides said we were still not halfway to the next village. Something was wrong. The tracks wove in and out, crossing and recrossing. Once when we approached a watercourse, some large animal stirred in the reeds and hurried off northwards. Was it elephant or tiger? I gripped the sabre tight. It had stayed dramatically by my side since that day I set out alone from Cuty. We needed water to cook rice, but the next two streams were dry. This was becoming the kind of forced march which I had managed to avoid since the long trudge from Pim's village to Pleiku. Tripping and slipping, it was hard to keep up with the guides. Once when we stopped, I got out the compass. It was almost the first time I had used it. Our route had been east–west for nearly a month, and on a lost path we must follow the same bearing. The guides' instinct turned out to be correct. In pitch darkness and an overgrown wood we were still heading west. If we missed the village, a westward march would bring us in the fullness of time to the banks of the River Mekong. Meanwhile we looked out for a clearing in which to spend the night, then suddenly after eight hours in the forest a light shone in the darkness out in front. We had reached our destination.

I shall never forget the reception they gave us at this particular village. Why were they so gay, never stopping to laugh and talk? First, the harvest was home – a bumper crop, enough to last twelve months until the next season. Second, the village was near enough Stung-Treng for the peasants to go to market three or four times a month. The people of this village were very poor, but so proud of the newly-harvested rice that they wanted me to sample a pot cooked, as it were, straight from the fields. One or two eggs were produced. In the enthusiasm, something went wrong with their cooking, and the whites turned out as hard as leather.

The morning after was the thirtieth morning of the journey, dawn of a day on which I hoped to reach Stung-Treng, the tiny Cambodian town described to me in advance by soldiers as 'zero'. Soon after first light, villagers led the way to the south bank of the Sre Pok river. For the next few hours we wended our way through richer and bigger riverside villages. At three in the afternoon we saw a sight which after this serio-comic crossing of the Indo-China plateau on foot was truly memorable. A spit of land nosed outwards from the north bank of the Sre Pok river. Another river lay beyond, but it did not look very big from this distance. We had reached the River Mekong at last. Before the war it was possible to travel by car from Binh-Dinh on the China Sea to Stung-Treng on the Mekong. At the time of my journey, a blocked frontier, a broken bridge, and abandoned roads made the journey impracticable except on foot. The early French explorers did it on horseback or by elephant. Their successors built roads and bridges which have since fallen into decay.

There lay the River Mekong in all its glory. The rise and fall of its waters had been the heartbeat of Cambodia since the days of Angkor and before. In a few months' time the snows would melt in Tibet and the River Mekong's swollen waters would once again transform Cambodia into a vast fish-pond. During the flood-season a watercourse linking the Mekong to an inland lake, the Great Lake, appears to flow backwards, taking the water up to the lake instead of down from it. This is because the flood-water of the River Mekong itself cannot escape quickly enough down to the delta. Fish swim up to the Great Lake and breed, but when the flood-water subsides they never escape back to the Mekong. The annual fish harvest is about 130,000 tons. Angkor was built near the shores of the Great Lake; and in theory an enemy navy could easily take it by surprise. The Chams did not know Ankgor could be reached by water till in A.D. 1177 a Chinese pilot showed them the way. They took Angkor by storm and sacked it. Later buildings show sculptured reliefs of naval battles between Chams and Khmers, some of which must have taken place on the River Mekong. A proverb about this great river points a way to the understanding of Cambodian life today. 'When the water rises,' says the proverb, 'fish eat the ants. When the water subsides, ants eat the fish.' Cambodia's future at this time depended on her neutrality, which rose and fell like the River Mekong, but never changed its essential character. As for pro-Russian fish and anti-Communist ants, they swam or crawled to office according to which way the waters of neutrality were running.

FOUR

West from the Mekong

CHAPTER SEVENTEEN

TREE-BARK SOUP

Stung-Treng stands at the parting of the ways. South lies the Cambodian plain. North there are the mountains of Laos, from which the River Mekong emerges as it wends its way south. One of its tributaries flows past the final resting-place of Henri Mouhot, the explorer. I decided to have two days' rest before going across the Mekong and continuing my journey. It was a change to be somewhere with a market. I bought some condensed milk and a tin of Australian butter, both of which had a disastrous effect on the stomach.

My talk with the Governor of Stung-Treng province was a success, mainly because he was due to retire from the Cambodian Civil Service in three weeks' time. He was hoping for an embassy post abroad. We talked in French, since I found this worked better with senior Cambodian officials. Previously I used to think that to address a man in his own language is invariably the best method of approach if you can speak it fluently, but French was more appropriate for high Cambodian officials, who liked speaking a European language. On the way down from the frontier through villages, knowledge of the Cambodian language had been of the utmost help. When people offered food and lodging, instead of using sign language, I was able to thank them with the words of traditional politeness which the humblest Cambodian habitually uses in everyday speech. Khmer, the Cambodian language, is not difficult to learn, since it has no tones like Chinese or Viet-Namese. Written Khmer is the same basically as it was in the

149

time of Angkor. Damp and insects have long since destroyed any palm-leaf books which might date back to early times, but many stone inscriptions have survived on the walls of ancient Khmer buildings. These inscriptions are written in Sanskrit and ancient Khmer, from which is descended the Cambodian language used for books and newspapers today. It has changed less than English since Chaucer, but in spite of this, few Cambodians can read the ancient version of their own language. Some have learnt it specially, and one is permanently resident in Paris as an expert in ancient and modern Khmer. The Cambodian alphabet is derived from India, but scholars are not certain which Indian writing influenced it most. There is only one difficulty when learning to read – vowels change their sound according to the consonant to which they are attached. This is not as difficult as it seems, because there are only two kinds of consonants, so that each written vowel has only two different sounds.

It turned out that the Governor of Stung-Treng had an inadequate knowledge of his own language when it came to writing me a letter of recommendation in Khmer. He scratched his head, tore up the half-written draft, and called in a secretary to finish it. He made up for his deficiency by speaking fluent Viet-Namese, and – something important for a governor of a province near Laos – he knew Lao. The Governor confirmed unwittingly that travel on foot was the safest way of crossing this part of Cambodia. His face and legs were covered with cuts and bruises from an accident a few days before. His vehicle was crossing a wooden bridge which collapsed, hurling car and passengers into the ravine.

He explained about the military training of peasants. 'These men,' he said, 'are being trained to be what we call *chivapols*, a kind of peasant army. Cambodians have never, in the past, been able to defend their villages from marauders. For several years we have been creating these *chivapols*, as we call them, and teaching them to defend themselves. The purpose of the scheme is to drive away pirates and rebels from the villages, and stop them pillaging houses and ricefields. You must understand that if Cambodia was invaded from outside, the country would not have a chance. All would be over in forty-eight hours.' My thoughts went back to the fifteen-year-old girl sloping arms in the warbling forest. One day she would be a doughty *chivapol*. I hoped for Cambodia's sake that the *chivapols* would not use their newly found skills to become pirates.

'Hygiene,' went on the Governor. 'That's one of my chief problems. I cannot get these people to boil water before drinking. You see what happens. They drink from any old stream, and bang, two days later, they're down with dysentery.' I thought back over the journey so far. Obliged to drink nine or ten pints of liquid a day, I had drunk water in nearly every hamlet from the frontier to Stung-Treng. Though I had caught dysentery only once, I always feared the consequences of drinking from these tainted water supplies, and was forever thinking that the morrow would bring some fatal disease. So far I had been lucky.

At this moment, the door flew open and a man knelt down in the corridor outside. 'Come in,' said the Governor. 'Stand up. I'm not a Prince.' The man was a Communist soldier who had come out of the forest to accept the amnesty offered by the Cambodians. He was Laotian by birth and could not speak Cambodian. I admired the speed with which his case was handled. He was given permission to stay in Stung-Treng for fifteen days, during which time he must establish proof that he was born and domiciled in Cambodia. If not, he would be sent back to Laos. Although the War had been over nearly four years, many pro-Viet-Minh Communists were still at large.

I had been too hopeful in expecting to find traces of an ancient Khmer road on the east bank of the Mekong. On the west bank we were about to enter a region of forests where hundreds of Khmer ruins lie hidden from view. This was likely to be the terrain where my search might well be rewarded. I was still only in the fifth week of my journey, so it looked as though I might reach Angkor in well under ten. We rowed across the River Mekong in mid-afternoon. Where the River Sre Pok joined it, there was a rich fishing ground. As we passed, the cylindrical wicker baskets were hauled up, revealing handsome fish leaping in the air as they gasped for breath. The Chinese boat-owner stopped to buy one of the larger fish. In the market on the far bank it could be resold for twice the price he paid here. It took an hour to cross the river, which shone like silver as afternoon turned to evening.

The land of milk and butter was far behind already. Supper that night was rice, fish, and tree-bark soup. The District Officer sent me to stay in a kind of dosshouse for travellers. Luckily, the inmates all came from the village to which I was heading the next day, so there was no difficulty in finding guides. Tree-bark soup is not as unappetizing as it sounds. The bark was tough and tasteless, made edible by the addition of salt and herbs. It was better than no soup at all. Several kinds of trees could be used. One of the best was *kaki*, a wood also popular for making boats and houses. Into this peaceful supper-party erupted a character from what I can best describe as a Cambodian version of the *Canterbury Tales* – to wit, a village clerk. He shouted at the top of his powerful voice, and continued to do so in bed, where he carried on a kind of soapbox discourse through the bamboo wall. Despite the fact that I had come directly from the District Officer, it seemed that one important person had not been informed. That was him – the clerk.

He settled himself in the middle of the floor with a pile of papers wrapped in last year's Cambodian calendar. He was in no hurry to reach the point – whatever the point was – and flicked over the papers, casually referring to their contents. Finally, he produced a new-looking Cambodian book. There were so many words derived from the Pali language in its title that I could not for the moment say what it was. The clerk started preaching on a text drawn from the book. He used nearly every catchword in day-to-day Cambodian political jargon. The first of these was 'Neutrality' – a word which has an historical sense for us, but little for the Cambodians. One of the worst bricks which could then be dropped in 'neutral Cambodia' was to refer to her neutrality as 'neutralist' – another catchword right out of favour. This beloved Cambodian word 'neutrality' described something newly acquired, but not yet understood. Neutrality was a kind of magic, treasured and worn round the neck like a potent talisman. Knowing all this, I listened to the garbled remarks of the clerk.

'This book,' he said, 'is about neutrality. France, England, China, Russia, Spain, and Cambodia. These are the countries which have so far "got" neutrality.' What was he talking about? Then another hackneyed word came tumbling out – 'independence'. 'Our country has only just become independent,' announced the clerk. 'That means our knowledge is very small, but we are learning every day.'

True enough – nearly every Cambodian would tell you the same.

Later he asked me: 'Are there wild animals in England?'

'No,' I replied. 'There are not very many.'

'Yes, yes,' he cried. 'Countries that have been independent a long time kill off their wild animals. We in Cambodia realize this. Take France, for example. There are hardly any wild animals

153

in France. That's why our government controls the number of people who go shooting wild game.' The reader should not be surprised if this sounds like a series of *non sequiturs*. For the Cambodians, 'independence' was a kind of *non sequitur* itself, in which they blindly (but not mistakenly) put their faith. Then the clerk added ambiguously: 'A few months ago, my men snared a Frenchman hunting elephant without a permit. He swiped a pair of tusks before we caught him. They hate us being independent.'

The conversation then turned to the subject of Prince Norodom Sihanouk, the ex-King. This happened to be a time of lacuna in Cambodian politics – the Prince out of public life, just about to make a comeback by public request. The phrase used by these villagers when referring to the Prince meant, in plain English, 'the King'. 'When is the King coming back?' they complained. 'We were told the King was coming back last week. But he hasn't come.' They called Prince Sihanouk 'The King' though he had resigned the monarchy several years earlier. This act provoked the West to compare him with Shaw's King Iviagnus, for ex-King Sihanouk formed his own political party and won every seat at the elections. But the common people still regarded him as king. Not only did they refer to him as king, they continued to worship and love him as Kings of Cambodia have been loved and worshipped by their subjects for many centuries. I supposed part of the reason was that the actual king, Suramarit, the Prince's father, was old, and would rarely be seen in villages and remoter parts of the country. In contrast to his father, Prince Sihanouk was famous for his journeys into the most distant hamlets of the *petit peuple* – his own favourite French description of the Cambodian peasantry. They would always be his most loyal supporters. They worshipped the clothes he wore and the things he touched. There were three personages in Cambodia who had to be addressed

For the *petit peuple* he had been and would always be 'the King'

with the royal language only used before royalty. They were –
the King, the Queen, and the ex-King. As ex-King, Prince
Sihanouk held a position which had always been highly regarded
in Cambodian history. He had the special title of *Upayuvareach*
for which the French equivalent was *Monseigneur*. Educated and
politically conscious Cambodians referred to the Prince by his
correct title. Newspapers and the radio also got it right. For the
petit peuple he had been and would always be 'the King'. His
name had been added to Cambodian history books as one of
the great Cambodian kings. Today the schoolchildren learn that
Angkor the Great was built by Jayavarman the Seventh, but,

155

before they reach the chapter in which this is described, there is a preface in which they read that the new Cambodia is being built by ex-King Prince Norodom Sihanouk Varman. Like his forefathers, Prince Sihanouk bears the extra title of 'Varman', which means 'Protector'. Reports in Western newspapers have built up images of the Prince as a mercurial saxophone-playing politician. I met him for an interview after the journey described in this book, and found I was talking to an intelligent statesman in the prime of life, who could express himself in several languages with great force and charm.

CHAPTER EIGHTEEN

BUDDHIST EXPERIMENT

The new guides were rather odd. The young one, very goofy-looking, was thirty-two. The old-looking one said he was only nineteen. They had worked fifteen days on a road-building project for the Cambodian Public Works department. Wages amounted to three hundred riels, with which they were very satisfied. Part had already been spent on clothes, a belt, exercise-books, tobacco, alcohol, and other provisions. It was a good day's walk through the forest to the next village. Most of the streams were dry, for the Cambodians have less knowledge of hydraulics than their ancestors, the ancient Khmers. We had some mandarin oranges which I had bought in the market. They were very sweet. The younger guide carefully wrapped up the pips in a piece of paper.

'To plant round my house,' he said.

They had been drinking the night before, I guessed. Groans, splutters, hiccoughs, and chokings continued for more than ten kilometres. For the first time in Cambodia I saw a wild deer. It stood near us on the path, then went bounding away into the forest. On a stretch of grassy plain two cranes rose up majestically and perched on a distant tree. Ox-carts were going in the opposite direction to us. Loaded with rice and new raffia sacks, they had come from a village three nights away. The contents of each cart would fetch three or four hundred Cambodian riels from a Chinese dealer at the market.

On the outskirts of the next village, there was a little hut on the right of the track, which the people called the House of the Neak

Ta. There are all kinds of local spirits which Cambodians call *Neak Ta*. The most famous *Neak Ta* are images in the Chinese temples of the Cambodian capital. Once a year, they are cleaned and taken in procession round the streets of the capital for a parade in front of the Royal Palace. The village had a monastery school which had been going for four years. The teachers were Buddhist monks. The monastery schools of Cambodia have an interesting history which shows that though the French had good ideas, their attitude to Cambodia sometimes delayed the ideas being deployed successfully.

In the early years of this century two Frenchmen realized that Cambodia's Buddhist monasteries were the traditional centres of popular education. They had the idea of renovating some of the then defunct monastery schools, but several cardinal mistakes were made. Lay teachers were installed in what had always been a stronghold of Buddhist monks, and another mistake was to put the French language on the curriculum. However, the experiment was partially successful for a time, though these two experimenters were by themselves in the wilderness of colonial administration. Their successors were apathetic, and the results were not followed up. A long time passed before the experiment was tried again. This was in the 1920s, when money spent on improving education in Cambodia was poured down the drain with very little result. It was all the more frustrating for the French, because their education policy in neighbouring Viet-Nam was doing well.

The job of renewing the experiment was given to Louis Manipoud, today the doyen of Cambodian-speaking Frenchmen. To him the scheme owed its success, although foundations were laid before he took over. This is what Manipoud wrote to justify his work. He was one of those rare birds in a French colony who learnt the language of the people, and thoroughly understood what he was doing.

'The foreign [i.e. French] nature of our teaching policy [he wrote] sterilizes the brain. Nothing in Cambodia can blossom if we do not weigh up sufficiently in our minds the importance of Buddhism and the importance of the monks. Wanting to separate a Cambodian from his monks is to make the gravest of miscalculations.'

Yet, this was precisely what his predecessors had done in bringing French-language instruction into the monasteries together with teachers who were not Buddhist monks.

A guinea-pig province was chosen for the experiment. Head monks were consulted about the project and their support actively wooed. A suitable monastery was chosen as a training-college for the monk student-teachers who were destined to run the renovated schools. An experienced teacher was put in charge, and the first students recruited from surrounding monasteries. Some of them failed to make the grade, but those who passed did so with flying colours. The graduating monks returned to their monasteries and reopened or inaugurated monastery schools. Hours of study were so arranged as not to interfere with the monk-teacher's religious and devotional life. The schools multiplied and were popular with the villagers, who could now have their children taught to read and write. One teaching centre was not enough. Under Manipoud's guidance new centres were started and the scheme snowballed successfully. The five-hundredth school was opened by the King of Cambodia only eleven years after the pilot scheme began. Four years later nearly forty thousand children were attending more than nine hundred schools. Half of those taking examinations passed. This was all a triumph for Manipoud and his loyal helpers. The French Colonial Government was pleased because the scheme cost very little to run. In 1937 the cost per child was only a fraction of what it cost to educate them elsewhere.

To return to my journey, this monastery school, which I then visited in the middle of the forest, was a direct descendant of Manipoud's 1923 experiment. Thanks to Frenchmen like him, education was reaching the remoter villages of Cambodia's most backward province in 1957. The day proved to be an educational outing. I often heard myself being described wrongly as an English envoy sent on tour by the King of Cambodia himself. Now, for the first time, I acted on His Majesty's behalf – as postman. Two school textbooks were being sent to a distant village. We had to bear them hence. They were not intended for use by schoolchildren, but were part of Prince Norodom Sihanouk's campaign against adult illiteracy. Orders had gone out to the provinces that adults – eighteens to sixties – should be taught to read. Each village was tackling the problem in its own way. At this village there were twice-monthly night classes attended by between sixty and seventy adults. At another village there were night classes every day during the summer months. Thirty or forty adults attended. I was impressed, and frankly surprised, to find a Cambodian Government policy being vigorously carried out in such a remote corner of the kingdom. I asked the teacher if the adults liked coming. 'Yes,' he said. 'They like learning about independence, neutrality, and all that.' So these were the two words which figured prominently in the beginners' reading lessons, those two old political war-horses which I knew so well, 'neutrality' and 'independence'.

Off we went through the woods, bearing the books in a parcel tied with jungle twine. There were frequent signs of wild elephants – flattened corridors of grass and steaming dunghills. Peacocks and wild monkeys were the only wild life we saw. Since leaving the banks of the River Mekong, I had prepared a new answer to the question 'Where are you going?'

'Angkor,' I replied, and then waited.

'Angkor,' they said. 'We've heard of Angkor, but we know nothing about it.'

This was rather a shock. Angkor might, for all they knew, be the name of a vegetable or a boat. I had always thought that every Cambodian knew something about Angkor, if only enough to say that the ancient Khmers were a great race of warriors and builders. Most Cambodians have heard of two Angkors, which they call Little Angkor and Big Angkor. Little Angkor is a somewhat inappropriate name for Angkor Wat, whereas Big Angkor is Angkor the Great, the city of Jayavarman the Seventh.

'Angkor?' said one peasant. 'A good, happy place, so they say.'

'Can you tell me why?' I asked.

'There are lots of people at Angkor,' he replied. 'And wherever Cambodians find lots of people, they always say that place is happy.'

He had put his finger on the most typical of Cambodian national characteristics.

We made a detour to visit a village, where yet another tribe, the Pear, were supposed to live. There seemed very little difference between them and the Cambodians except that they had an extra language which they talked among themselves. Their houses were different, some not built on Cambodian stilts at all.

'These people are Kouy,' said one of the Cambodian guides. 'Are you Kouy?' I asked a woman in Cambodian.

'I don't know,' she said. 'I may be Pear, and I may be Kouy.'

'Are you Cambodian?' I asked.

'Oh, yes,' she replied. Of course I'm Cambodian.' Both Pear and Kouy are thoroughly intermarried with the Cambodians. They believe in Buddhism if there is a monastery in the district, and are much more Cambodianized than the Pnong on the east side of the Mekong. One of the Pears, or he may have been a Kouy, told me about an ancient stone on the banks of a nearby stream. It was difficult to get an exact description except that the people in the next village often passed it in their ox-carts. At the next village it took some time before they understood what stone I was talking about. When they grasped the point, they became quite excited and said the stone had some Siamese characters on it. I was hoping for relics of an ancient Khmer bridge, or rest-house, which would establish the presence of the ancient Khmer road to Champa in this region. Equally exciting would be an unknown ancient Khmer inscription, perhaps giving information about the road.

When the sun became less hot, two villagers volunteered to lead me to the stone. It was said to lie near a track leading to another village. After half an hour we turned right down a dry water-course. Ten minutes later, this stream joined a bigger stream. The banks of the two streams rose slightly to form an eminence. There was no sign of a ruined bridge or rest-house, only a stone which from this distance looked like an English milestone, and could well be an ancient Khmer inscription. No luck – whatever writing the stone once bore had disappeared, and its surface crumbled in our hands. My own guess was that this stone marked the boundary of a land concession during the time when foreigners occupied this part of Cambodia. It was probably less than a hundred years old. It was disappointing not to find something more interesting. One of the villagers said the stone had been growing taller every year. We scratched away some earth from round the base of the stone, leaving it slightly more exposed than before. Next time the villagers passed in their ox-carts, they would be able to wag their heads as usual and say that the stone was still growing taller. We returned to the village, where the headman's wife served a good chicken soup. It tasted delicious after our exertions.

CHAPTER NINETEEN

LOST

The next morning, a muscle in my left thigh seemed swollen, and making any movement of the leg was painful. I must have strained it scrambling about in those watercourses the evening before. Previous experience of strained muscles told me that they sometimes stay swollen for weeks. It might be months before the thigh returned to normal size. By rough reckoning we still had about one hundred and fifty miles to go before reaching Angkor. However, I tried to forget that the thigh was hurting, as the guides set off as usual. There were good paths through the forest. Sometimes we crossed open heathland. The ox-carts had sets of bells, and we could hear their Arcadian tinkling far away in the forest. Their cadences reminded me of Pim's gongs. The children carried hunting-horns and blew broken snatches as they wandered through the woodlands.

'Does the sound of horns mean anything?' I asked.

'No,' the people answered. 'The young ones blow them just for fun.'

The people here seemed less Cambodian and more Kouy, or Pear. Their houses, built on stilts, were square, one side open for cooking and the other closed for sleeping and storing rice. The atmosphere of Arcadia was complete when an old man told me the story of his youth, how he used to rove through the forest looking for wild honey. Then, the moment for which I had been waiting. Deep in the woods, remembered the old man, there was a ruined tower, not far from the deserted village of Knifehandle.

The old man had lived at Knifehandle when he was a boy, so had one of his friends. After questioning, it seemed likely that they must have last seen the tower fifty years ago, about the time when that French infantry officer (see p. 25) was making his inventory of ancient Khmer monuments. 'No Frenchmen have ever seen it,' said the old man dramatically. 'Once the Siamese came there, but they could not understand the strange writing on the stones.'

All this sounded hopeful, but, though there were more than nine hundred ancient Khmer ruins and sites, it was no part of my scheme to visit any but a few. At this point we were less than a hundred miles from a known section of the ancient Khmer road to Champa near Prah Khan. We were still on the uncertain section of the map, which did not mark Knifehandle or the stream near which the ancient Khmer tower was supposed to stand. The old man was doubtful whether he could find the way after so many years. He was afraid that if we took a long time to find the ruins it would be impossible to reach the next village before nightfall. Formerly, there was another village half-way, but like Knifehandle it had been abandoned. In the evening after making preparations for the expedition, the villagers killed a chicken for supper – one half was roast and the other stewed. The method of killing was strictly Kouy (or Pear). A ten-year-old boy fitted an arrow to his crossbow and shot the bird plumb in its breast. At a distance of twelve yards the arrow went right through and stuck out the other side, transfixing the fowl and showing the power of the bow. My left thigh was still in bad order, and the whole leg was now inflamed. It seemed as though every tendon and cartilage was protesting on behalf of the damaged muscle. The inside edge of the knee felt as if it had been tapped with a hammer. The ankle was in steel handcuffs. The thigh, itself, although red, did not seem any more swollen than on the day before. I feared the guides might lose confidence in my ability to make the march, let alone find a lost tower near a deserted village. What I feared most was a fall. With one lame leg, it was much easier to trip and fall, hurting the other leg or making the lame one worse. I hobbled round the village. If they looked carefully, the villagers could have seen that my left leg was swinging backwards without taking any strain.

It rained in the night, unusual for the month, so the jungle was wet underfoot. We soon left behind any vestiges of heath. The path led north-west over a tree-clad hill. If in the past I had always been able to keep pace with the guide, now I lagged behind miserably. Simple things, such as stepping over a fallen log or scrambling down the slippery bank of a stream, became awkward obstacles to progress. Although abandoned, however, the path was not too overgrown. We stopped once for some rice, and reached the appointed stream after four hours. The abandoned village of Knifehandle lay somewhere to the north. The guides indicated several impenetrable-looking paths which were supposed to lead there. Undergrowth and tall rain-trees shaded the banks of our stream, but where was the ruined tower?

'I don't know,' said the old man. 'This was open country when I was a boy. Look at it now.' We hid the baggage near the stream and set off northwards along the west bank. There was no track. Sometimes it was easier to wade through the water. The guides went ahead. I followed slowly at first through shallows, then deep pools where the water lapped refreshingly against my bruised thigh. The guides waited, and we all moved on together. After fifteen minutes the old man turned west and struck off into the jungle. The tower, he said, was somewhere among the nearby hillocks. Before going far, he announced, to my surprise, that we were already standing on the dried-up site of the sacred pool, so often found near ancient Khmer buildings. The reader will remember how important the building of waterworks was to the ancient Khmers. 'The tower should be on one of these hills,' the guide said. We looked where he pointed, in front, then to the direction from which we had come. I guessed that the hidden temple lay behind us, somewhere to the south of the pool. Leaving one guide as marker, I returned with the other to the hillock we had just passed. Sure enough, when we looked more closely, we could distinguish the ruins of an ancient Khmer building. It was gripped by the jungle in that characteristic way so well known to anyone who has seen Angkor itself. In my first enthusiasm I identified the site as a ruined rest-house on my ancient Khmer road from Angkor to Champa. It seemed to have the right kind of sanctuary, with another smaller ruin which might have been remains of the porch. The nave in between would have disappeared. Proportions seemed to be correct.

On closer inspection I found that the building was anything but an ancient Khmer rest-house. There were two separate towers. One was oblong and had an entrance on the north side. Nearby, to the north-west, there was a smaller tower with an entrance on the east side. The guide told me it was called the Young Daughter's Tower, I could not find out the legend of the young daughter, except that she had been a daughter of the king. There were pieces of ancient Khmer sculpture lying inside the precinct wall. One was a lion with compressed haunches and an upright trunk, like the stone lions at Angkor. Lions have never made their habitat in Cambodia, so sculptors had to get their designs from abroad. Over the centuries there was little artistic development in the form of a Khmer lion. Among the other pieces there was an early statue of a human figure. The head, feet, and right leg were missing. The body was strongly interpreted and incised with plunging thigh-lines to indicate drapery.

We looked unsuccessfully for the writing which the Siamese had not been able to understand. This kind of story gets told about any ruins deep in the jungle which nobody can remember visiting for a long time. The wall surrounding the two towers was easy to trace, and the total enceinte ran to sixty-five yards square. Trees were growing out of the masonry. The old man was pleased to have found the tower so quickly. Bearing in mind its position relative to the old cart-tracks and abandoned villages, I expected to find it mentioned in one of the French itineraries or in the infantry captain's inventory. We went back to the stream and retrieved our baggage from the bushes. The leg which had survived marching thus far was very stiff. I was afraid it would seize up altogether.

Thick undergrowth and high jungle grass made it difficult to find which way the old cart-track was leading. After a fruitless search for three-quarters of an hour, the guides admitted they were lost. Nor did they find the way for the rest of the day. For the next six hours we had a gruelling trek, one which I would not like to repeat. The jungle was pleasant enough as long as one stayed on a well-defined path, but we had lost the path. Now we had to scramble across overgrown watercourses and cut a way through tangled bamboo thickets and high jungle grasses. Sometimes we seemed to strike an elephant path. It would not be so much a path as a corridor created by the passing once only of a dozen wild elephants. For twenty or thirty metres the going would be good, then back into the undergrowth. We curved in and out, going now north and now south trying to find the abandoned track. Once we found an elephant track which led more than a kilometre across a narrow strip of plain. It led in the right direction – west. The guides used their intuition. After several hours one of them led off in a wide arc and headed due east, if he had but realized it, towards the ancient kingdom of Champa. The sun was high in the sky, hidden behind clouds. He had lost his tracker's sense of direction. I stopped the march and proved by compass that we were walking back on our tracks.

My own idea was to march due west. If we did not hit a village we should eventually come to a broad north–south stream, the Stung Sen. Tributaries of the Stung Sen ran east–west. It was possible to walk between them and parallel to them without crossing them, thus regaining lost bearings. So began a compass march more tiring than any of our wanderings during the past hours. The march took us from fixed point to fixed point. We climbed useless hills and cut a way through superfluous over-grown valleys. Out in front ran a herd of 'kting' as the guides called them, about twenty strong. They were like domestic water-buffaloes, but browner and shaggier. I wondered what the French word for this animal was. Could it be the gaur? Conversation with hunters had taught me to respect the gaur as one of the prized pieces of game which the Cambodian forest has to offer. Once when we climbed a hill higher than the others there was a sound of trumpeting elephants just in front. I asked the guides if we would see any of the herd. They said that wild elephants are frightened of humans and prefer running away into the forest. The trumpeting continued. Sometimes it seemed as if the elephants were throwing a cordon round our hill. Screeches came from all sides at once, but we saw nothing.

After crossing thinner jungle we came to a forest drinking-pool. It was muddy from animals that had recently been there in search of water. We saw none of them. Late in the after-noon we reached a stream, one of the tributaries of the Stung

Sen. The water had stopped running, and a dead pig lay on the gravel. Its body spread a foul smell. One of the guides was clutching a dead stag's antler, white with age. He had found it in the forest. As we followed the stream north-west and west, there were deep pools which had to be waded through. We were walking downstream according to the guides, but there was no current in the pools, which were stagnant. Soon they deepened, sometimes forcing us on to the bank, which towered above and had to be climbed at great exertion. Between the pools there were heaps of boulders, drifted sand, and sliding gravel. The stream twisted and turned. Sometimes it seemed to retrace its own course and lead back towards the east. Then we tried leaving its watercourse and ploughing through the jungle, but the bed of the stream was usually preferable. As the water became deeper, we had to carry the baggage on our heads. The only comforting thought was that this stream would lead to the broad Stung Sen, along whose banks there must be Cambodian villages.

At nightfall we were still lost. The guides wanted to continue although it was dark. After a time they stopped and cleared a space to light a fire on the edge of the forest. When the fire began to blaze, I attempted to dry clothes wet from wading in the stream. Our diet of rice and salt had never tasted better. I ate my way through nine bowls, only stopping to have them refilled. When night was on us and the guides had gone to sleep by the fire, I listened to the sounds of the forest. It had not been part of my plan to sleep out in the bush far from human habitation. My thoughts turned to the solitary traveller, Henri Mouhot, who almost one hundred years before had sat under just such a tree as this with its ganglious branches blotting out the night sky. In his diary he wrote:

'I have written these few notes on Cambodia after returning from a long hunting expedition, by the light of a torch, seated on my tiger-skin. On one side of me is the skin of an ape stripped off; on the other, a box of insects waiting to be arranged and packed. My desire is not to impose my opinions on anyone, especially with regard to the wonderful architectural remains which I have visited, but simply to disclose the existence of these monuments, which are certainly the most gigantic, but also to my mind display a more perfect taste than any left to us by the ancients. But after all, my principal object is natural history, and with that study I chiefly occupy myself.'

I knew this passage almost by heart, and regretted as I sat in the wild Cambodian forest that I had not yet found any wonderful architectural remains which I too could disclose to the world. Near by troupes of wild pigs were rustling and grunting in the undergrowth. We had disturbed them having a drink at the stream. My two Cambodian guides were fast asleep. Before going to sleep myself, I recalled that the day was Sunday, ninth day of the waxing moon, first of December, thirty-sixth evening of my journey from the coast to Angkor.

The next morning we continued to follow the stream down its tortuous course. Fallen trees and undergrowth barred the way frequently. Precipitous banks were climbed and long detours made through the forest. After two hours the guides said they recognized a track which could be seen descending into the water from the right-hand bank. The watercourse would lead us in time to a village, but if we took the track, they said, we could probably make it in less than three hours. Sitting down on the shingle, we breakfasted jubilantly off salt and rice. The time estimate proved wrong. Fifty minutes' brisk walk was enough. The villagers welcomed us in a wooden *sala*, the modern equivalent of an ancient Khmer rest-house. Like all Cambodian houses, it stood on firm wooden stilts some six feet off the ground. The floor was made of bamboo struts and the roof thatched with palm-leaves. Mats were brought from a nearby house, and after removing our footwear we settled ourselves comfortably on them. This is the normal way of receiving guests in a Cambodian village. There were, of course, no chairs, though you will see plenty in the houses of town-dwellers. Another meal was served, and we soon forgot the smell of rotting pig and the deserted path from Knifehandle. My thigh was better.

CHAPTER TWENTY

THE FLOWER FESTIVAL

'What about Angkor?' I asked.

'Angkor?' replied one man. 'That's a place where you see writing which no Cambodian can read. I have never been to Angkor, nor have I heard any stories about it.'

In answer to my usual questions, a second man surprised me by describing a Khmer bridge on the ancient north-west road in a different part of Cambodia altogether. This road formerly linked Angkor with an outpost of the ancient Khmer empire, now in Thailand (Siam). My informant had once travelled to the district in search of timber. That a 'local' should undertake such a long journey was a sign that we were emerging from the wilds at last.

Early in the afternoon we reached the banks of the Stung Sen. It was a broad stream, as I expected – the biggest obstacle which the ancient Khmer road would have had to cross between Angkor and the River Mekong. No traces of an ancient Khmer bridge have yet been found. Hamlets along the Stung Sen were potentially prosperous, but they were suffering from an almost total loss of the rice crop. The villagers could be seen reaping the pitiful remains of damaged crops. The lucky ones might save a sixth. Others could save nothing. Already in a season when rice should have been plentiful they were short of food for their daily meals. The Cambodian Government used to bring official aid to genuinely distressed areas. This aid took the form of rice – perhaps fifty kilograms for a household.

173

This sounded a good deal, but where there were ten mouths to feed it disappeared before the end of three days. In smaller families it still could not last very long. Rice was eaten three times a day, the meals being known, quite simply, as 'morning rice', 'midday rice', and 'evening rice'. I asked the Government's representative how the people would survive during the next twelve months. Could they work as labourers for the public works department? No luck, for in this district there was no new road under construction.

'They will have to live on roots and wild potatoes,' I was told. 'It is difficult for them, because these plants do not grow near the villages. They will have to go twenty or thirty kilometres from here and find them in the forest.' The forest was the direction from which we had come. Cambodians do not keep breath in body by eating roots normally, but in these poorer districts, when the rice-crop failed and the Government's aid was consumed, there was nothing else left to eat. The reason for the rice failure here was lack of water during the planting season. Some districts had also suffered from flooding. I asked about fish. They should have been able to catch plenty in the Stung Sen, but they did not seem to know how. They had no fishing-nets and traps like those we had seen on the River Mekong earlier in the journey.

The peasant life in this region was typical – like an antique pitcher with a myriad cracks. The thing which holds the pieces of the pitcher together is Buddhism. In these near-to-famine villages I had the good luck to see the peasants organize a Buddhist festival. A drum was beating in the distance, signal for the people to assemble for the fête. This Flower Festival, as it was called, was a purely Buddhist occasion at which the laity offered a flower to the Buddha together with a sum of money raised by public subscription. The money would be used by the monks for a building project at the monastery. I stayed that night in the house of the Festival President, who was also the village headman. He was counting out money when I arrived. Name of subscribers, and amounts, were entered scrupulously in an exercise-book. The President donated two hundred riels himself – about two pounds. Though corruption is rampant in Cambodia, and openly admitted by members of the Assembly in public debate, money contributed to a Buddhist cause never finds its way into the wrong hands. The reason for this is that most Cambodians are fervent Buddhists, more than in name only. They are terrified of going to Buddhist Hell. This hell is imagined by their painters and writers with a horror which reminds one of Brueghel or Jerome Bosch.

Soon we were joined by three old men dressed in white collarless blouses and black trousers, the correct male dress for a Buddhist festival in Cambodia. The three men had been chosen from among elders of the Buddhist laity to act as honorary masters of ceremony, known as *achars*. This role is often given to someone who has spent many years as a Buddhist monk, and knows the drill. In Cambodia no stigma attaches to any monk who leaves the yellow robe, whether after weeks, months, or years. It is one of the time-honoured customs of the country that the monks should be free to become laymen again whenever they wish. This freedom to enter and leave the order acts as a kind of safety-valve – one of the reasons why the Cambodian clergy are among the best disciplined of any in the Buddhist world, Buddhists from the other 'Little Vehicle' countries find with surprise that discipline is better regulated among Cambodian monks than among their own. Here are the comments of a Burmese monk published in a Rangoon newspaper:

'In Cambodia it is not possible for anyone who has committed a serious crime to enter the order. After taking the ordination, a new monk is given by his preceptor an identity card or certificate which bears the name of his ordination. It is the duty of every monk or novice to carry this card wherever he goes. If a monk is found to be doing something that should not be done by him, a policeman asks for his card and interrogates him. He is then, in the case of a minor misdemeaour, sent to his preceptor, who admonishes him to refrain from doing anything that is detrimental to the Buddhist religion in the future. For these reasons an immoral monk or novice is almost unheard of in Cambodia.'

'Why are you holding a festival?' I asked the *achars*.

'There is no special reason,' they answered. 'We have one from time to time, and collect money for the Buddhist monks. They're building a wooden house at the monastery, and hope to have it finished before the Cambodian New Year. The pillars were sunk last month.'

The total cost of the building would be between ten and twenty thousand riels (£100–200). Donating a house to Buddhist monks is one of the most approved ways in which Buddhist merit can be acquired by alms-giving.

Several hours after dark the drum was still beating. We walked two kilometres across the ricefields. I tried to guess what kind of monastery they were leading me to. Would it be one of those big and prosperous-looking places filled with gentry from all over the province? No, it had been founded only a short time. A few statues of Buddha were sheltered beneath a roof which rested on the traditional wooden columns. All four sides were open to the weather. There was no hard floor, only sand. Leaf-shaped stones, called 'seima' stones, surrounded the temple, limiting the space inside which the ceremonies might be validly held. This poor monastery owned a few tawdry mats, which had all been brought out and laid in the temple covering the centre of the building. Children ran to and fro playing in the shadows. Their feet dug up the sand, which flew into our nostrils and settled on the mats till they were just as sandy as anywhere else. The congregation was not composed of the provincial gentry, but the poorest of the poor peasants. I watched them as they filed in from the ricefields and clustered round the temple. The men were farmers in dusty black blouses and trousers. Their faces were a rich brown – the mark of a real Cambodian. These men were the direct descendants of Angkor's builders. The women carried one, sometimes two, children in their arms. They had brought their own mats and sat down on the edge of the sand. Babies screamed. As each mother suckled her young one, the noise subsided.

At this stage there was no light in the temple except for the moon, now waxing towards its fullness. Fifty yards away, the monastery *sala* was lit by a single hurricane lamp. Never more forcibly had the true Cambodia planted itself before my eyes. Here were the poorest and humblest of 4½ million Cambodians. Into the heart of Cambodia must always mean into the heart of Buddhist Cambodia. The treasurers were counting the money. Every few minutes an old man or woman would crawl respectfully to the centre of the temple and offer a crumpled banknote. If the almsgiver was unable to afford all of a five-riel note, he or she asked unashamedly for change. One treasurer sorted out 'fives' and 'tens' and 'ones', making neat packets, which were checked by another and wrapped in newspaper. After the final count, 'hundreds' were wrapped up in a special cloth and placed in an offertory bowl. The final sum collected was three thousand, one hundred riels – about

£30. The hurricane lamp was brought across from the *sala* and hung over our heads from a meat-hook. The monastery gong was struck. The faithful stopped what they were doing and all faced the statues of Buddha. Nobody sat cross-legged – a sitting position reserved by Cambodians for eating. The gong sounded again. We bowed three times to Buddha. '*Namo Tassa*' was the first prayer. In countless other Buddhist gatherings throughout the world this basic Buddhist formula is repeated three times:

> *Namo tassa Bhagavato Arahato Samma Sambuddhassa.*
> (Praise to the Blessed One, the Perfect One, the fully Self-Enlightened One.)

These are the opening words, which I knew by heart and repeated in unison with the congregation of this Cambodian monastery. While the service continued, a light breeze gently stirred the leaves of the sugar-palms outside.

When preliminary prayers were over the master of ceremonies struck the gong once more. A boy was sent to give another beat on the monastery drum. This was a signal to the monks that the laity were ready to receive them in the temple. The monks are the servants of the Buddhist laity, the vital means whereby Buddha's merit can be acquired and shared, so the Cambodians believe. Woe betide the Cambodian monk who fails to answer the people's call to prayer. Still, the monks are dignified masters of their own destinies. After a suitable pause, they came stepping through the shadows. Their robes were an assortment of colours – yellows, saffron, some of a dark browny red. This last colour had been approved by the head monk of all Cambodia, but uniformity of colour is not strictly enforced.

As they entered the temple, each monk knelt down before a statue of Buddha and bowed three times. Then they turned

Monks sat in front and novices behind

to face the people, sitting in two rows. Monks sat in front and novices behind. At a Buddhist ceremony the joy is not bottled up, and there is no tension. Everyone is relaxed. The monks smoke and talk, often making jokes among themselves. Cordials and aerated waters are served if the laity can afford them. Prayers are interrupted and restarted if the recitation has not come up to public approval. Between times, the laity chat, exchange betel-nut, leaving and entering the temple at will. Sitting in the darkness on our right, I could see a group of white-robed women, practitioners of the Ten Buddhist precepts. Each had brought gifts of betel-nut and betel-leaves for the monks These women would stay all night at the monastery. Some would snatch an hour or two's sleep in the *sala*. In the morning they would join together in the preparation and offering of food.

Now one of the monks began to recite. He was sitting in the back row, and held up a fan in front of his face. This was a custom observed in many Cambodian monasteries to prevent the congregation remarking that X or Y monk was saying the prayers on any particular occasion. When he had finished and the appropriate responses were over, two preaching chairs were set up in the middle of the temple just in front of where we were sitting. The chairs were made of local wood and decorated with a few simple painted designs. In the Buddhist Institute of Cambodia in Phnom Penh, you can see a magnificent preaching-chair buttressed by the traditional decoration, a pair of lion's heads. Six or seven minutes elapsed while the *achars* went to elaborate pains arranging cushions and refreshments so that the preachers would be perfectly comfortable. Two novices had been given the job of preaching. They were looking wretched at the thought of the ordeal ahead. When the gong sounded, they stepped forward and settled themselves on the preaching-chairs. Legs were tucked underneath, but they took some time getting into a comfortable position, like cats curling up in front of ar fire. They both looked nervous. One kept wiping his face with a handkerchief. I could see that his eyes were moist with tears. When he was not wiping, his fingers fidgeted with a small leaf-wrapped cigar.

Before the sermon began, we listened to a speech by one of the notables from the next village. In the opening sentence he used two kinds of Cambodian phrases for 'I', one for a layman addressing a monk and the second for a humble man speaking to important people. There were many Pali words in his speech, which made it difficult to understand. 'The headman of X … ' he began, 'is the President of this subscription. Many people have joined together with him. This, indeed, is the quickest way in which we can reach holy Nirvana. Buddhism is our national religion. May all contributors to this festival increase their property, have many grandchildren, live in large houses, and have fine crops of rice. Let us all say "Sathu" together.' *Sathu* – so be it. The Buddhist word for Amen boomed out suddenly across the plain.

Cambodian Buddhist sermons are seldom like their Christian equivalents. The preacher recites a sacred text by heart, or reads from a palm-leaf book. If he is speaking by heart it is customary to hold palm-leaves in the hand, turning the pages regularly as though the speaker were actually reading from a sacred book. I had never before seen two preachers working at the same time. The gong sounded again. The right-hand novice began to speak.

'We are only young,' he said, 'Please forgive us if our discourse is not very long. If there are mistakes, please excuse us.'

He went on in the same manner for three or four minutes, then the left-hand novice made a similar appeal for our indulgence. We listened next to a Buddhist dialogue lasting about half an hour, in which one novice asked the other about different ways of giving Buddhist alms. His role was that of the inquiring layman, it seemed. Each of his questions ended with a set phrase. I did not understand the phrase at first, but it came so often that I asked one of the *achar* for a Cambodian translation, It turned out to be the Pali version of 'over to you'. The left-hand novice played the part of a wise elder. His answers were couched in high-sounding Pali phraseology, which I did not understand. Still nervous, he held up a fan to hide the tears on his cheek, but gradually became more confident as memory served him well.

Neither of the novices faltered. They remembered their lessons word perfect. Sometimes one of them would translate the Pali answer into Cambodian so that we could all understand the meaning. At one stage reference was made to the monastery building programme. Lay women, who outnumbered the men present, were instructed to ask their absent husbands to collect certain woods and bring them in from the forest. In this way great merit could be acquired. About three out of four Cambodians would never question the basic principle of Buddhist merit. After twenty minutes the novices were really in their stride. The young left-hand novice, playing the part of the elder, put in an aside which made everyone laugh. What he said, in Cambodian, was roughly this: 'Though I'm using a lot of long Pali words, you mustn't think that I'm a long-Pali-words kind of person myself.' This was a reference to certain Buddhist monks and laymen who are over-pedantic with their use of Pali language in everyday speech. The Pali language is the sacred language in which many Buddhist texts are written. Some of these texts have been translated into English and published by the Pali Text Society of London. This remark about the long Pali words came after a lengthy explanation full of Pali expressions. When the explanation was complete, the right-hand novice started off again.

'There is yet one other matter, oh master, on which we seek guidance.'

Whispers were audible round the temple.

'Will the sermon last all night?' I heard them say.

The young novice had an answer ready for every situation.

'Remember,' he said. 'We agreed our discourse would be short.'

By general consent the 'other matter' was left to be preached on another day. The dialogue ended with bangs on the drum, gong-beating, and a single ear-splitting rocket which detonated over the sugar-palms into the darkness. I have listened to many sermons in English churches which the audience would gladly have brought to a stop by common consent, or by the agreeable expedient of letting off a rocket in the organ-loft. The most popular text in Cambodia is the *jatalca,* which tells how King Vessentara gave away his children as alms to a beggar and gained great merit. Once a year, at least, this story is recited in its entirety by relays of preachers. The laity have to stay all day at the monastery, which they willingly do, since they like hearing their favourite story.

It was hard to assess the reactions of these villagers at seeing a strange European appear from nowhere for their festival. When they found they could talk to me in their own language, they assumed quietly that I was trying to do the same as them – acquire a modicum of Buddhist merit.

FIVE

The Road to Angkor

CHAPTER TWENTY-ONE

GOLD RUSH

The next morning two reluctant guides led me to the village of Rovieng. All was deathly quiet. Even the military sentry-box was deserted, and snores issued from the guard-house window. This little village with its formless two-kilometre line of houses has a special claim to fame. There seemed to be an abnormal number of Chinese merchants for such a small place. One of them was curing a leopard-skin. Another was buying – gold. For Rovieng is indeed the centre of Cambodian California. Has history ever witnessed a more leisurely gold-rush town? The gold-mines are not actually in Rovieng, the situation of which seemed to be a mistake. Intended by the French to be a market town, it lies on a never-completed road from central Cambodia to south Laos, between wooded hills and a waterless plain. The villages which we had just left behind were mostly within easy reach of a stream, but not Rovieng, the seat of the administration.

There was one thing at any rate to astonish the visitor – the local school. Twice a day the long characterless village street was filled with a great horde of schoolchildren going to and from their classrooms. Just as the sun was setting, they came out in single file, smiling silhouettes. In the background stood a sugar-palm, that unforgettable hallmark of the Cambodian landscape. Since independence, Prince Norodom Sihanouk had devoted much effort to the creation of secondary schools in the provinces. Rovieng was not one of these schools, but its children could graduate to a new college in the local provincial capital. As each year, passed, these colleges were increasing their number of classes by one, so that after six years there would be a complete set of classes from *première* to *sixième*.

Thanks to the hospitality of the District Officer, I was able to rest for several days in comfort. When next setting off, I hit the trail for the gold-mines. The first mine was on the side of a hill where iron had been worked by the French at an earlier date. There was a scene of astonishing inactivity. The huts were roofless, and uninhabited. A few Chinese were shaking gold-dust in dishes. Three or four men were digging. There was no gold seam, only the reddish pits open to the sky. Anyone was allowed to dig, as there was no official exploitation of the mine. I stopped three Cambodian miners who were on their way home, and asked them what had happened to the gold-rush. They said that the season for digging was over. Many of the miners had gone home to take in the rice-harvest. The gold could wait a few months – no hurry. The Cambodians would harvest the gold, all in their good Cambodian time. They showed me the booty of a day's digging. A tiny speck of gold was visible in the bottom of a little medicine bottle. If a miner worked hard the whole month, he might, if he was lucky, find gold worth four pounds sterling. This would be sold to the Chinese.

There were some odd rumours going about. According to one, Europeans were supposed to have concealed the presence of gold from the Cambodians. In the end they had been obliged to share the secret with two employees. In this way the secret leaked out round the district till all the locals learnt how to dig for gold. I was given a hut in which to spend the night. Underneath there was a pigsty occupied by three sows. They had arrived an hour after me and were travelling in the opposite direction. The next-door hut had been taken over by a travelling Buddhist monk.

A few Chinese were shaking gold-dust in dishes

Head of his monastery, he had been on a visit to a distant town, where he had spent the proceeds of a Buddhist festival. Not a sou remained – instead of cash, he now had wire-netting, nails, lumps of iron, and twenty-five bags of cement. All these materials were to be used to build a house for the monks at his monastery.

The gold-site where I spent this first night was preferred by some prospectors because it had a water-supply. After passing another sparsely populated mining village the next morning, we came to a gold seam on the north side of another hill. It ran east–west. This was the gold-rush for which I was looking. Several years passed after the war before the Cambodian Government gave permission for people to mine gold once more. The ban had been lifted earlier in the year of my visit. A rambling village had

189

grown up round the gold-seam. Even at this second hill it was the 'off' season. More than half the miners had gone back to their ricefields. A few hundred remained. I watched them working in groups up and down the seam – twenty, thirty, or fifty to a group. Ladders led into the depths, some into dark holes more than thirty metres deep.

One day's work in a group-pit produced so little earth that the spoils were not worth dividing. After ten days, or sometimes as many as thirty, a share-out took place, each member of the team receiving a small sack of earth. My arrival coincided with one of these share-outs. A noisy group of miners were arguing about the sacks. From out of the group came a file of men and women, each with a reddish sack on the shoulder. Some of them ran. When had I ever seen people in Cambodia run? Yes, they actually ran. It was disturbing to see the corrupting effect of gold on these simple folk. We stopped in our tracks as the diggers fought over the spoils and ran home quickly with what they won. Half an hour later they could be seen in their houses, shaking the earth and looking feverishly for scraps of gold.

No records were kept of output. After asking questions it seemed possible that about a hundred pounds worth of gold left the village every month. The buying price was fixed, but the selling price varied below a fixed ceiling. The middlemen were Chinese, one of whom told me that no Chinese merchant dared pay less than the fixed price when buying from the miners, for they were afraid of being beaten up. The wives of miners were very much in residence and wore little images of Buddha encased in gold from the mine. Cambodians love wearing gold, which forms an important part of the wedding trousseau. The village was unsavoury in more ways than one, for there was no water-supply. During the rainy season this had not mattered. When prospectors began arriving there had been ample time to dig wells, but in the rush for gold nobody had wanted to waste effort digging for water. Now the rains had stopped, everyone was complaining and trying to blame the authorities. Another effect of the gold was to make groceries a quarter more expensive than in the outside world. There had been several deaths from illness and one in the seam itself after a fall of earth. This was not surprising as the seam was only a hundred yards long and stopped abruptly at both ends. Diggers had to descend on rickety ladders deeper and deeper into the hill if gold was to be found. After the rice-harvest the population would increase again up to a thousand. I dreaded what would happen without a proper water-supply.

I asked the police whether they thought the atmosphere was ripe for brawling and killing. They replied that the diggers were Cambodians first and gold-miners second. They arranged share-outs according to their own rules and rarely came to blows. This un-Cambodian atmosphere had been disturbed the previous evening by arrival of the head monk of the province together with four other monks from his monastery. They had come to hold a Buddhist festival. The visiting monks were lodged in a gold-miner's shack, as there was no monastery. On all sides the sound of hammers could be heard. The miners were hammering gold – gold which a Buddhist monk is forbidden to touch.

I had no wish to see any more of Cambodia's gold-rush, nor the proposed Buddhist festival, which did not seem as sponta-neous as the one described in the previous chapter. The President of this gold-mine festival said he had received a letter from the Head Monk of all Cambodia. In this letter, which I did not see, the Head Monk was supposed to have told these villagers that they must hold a festival before the end of the month. The Head Monk of all Cambodia at this time was a much-travelled man, highly respected in Thailand, Burma, and Ceylon, where the people practise the same kind of Buddhism as in Cambodia. Although a Head Monk of all Cambodia is a spiritual leader and administrator, he does not have the kind of spiritual powers which the Pope exercises in the Roman Catholic Church, nor can he really be likened to an English archbishop. The active head of the Cambodian Buddhist Church is the King. When the King of Cambodia tells the Buddhist monks to do something they have to obey. At the time of my journey the Buddhist monks of Cambodia did not take part in politics, but since the most influential political leader was an ex-king, Prince Norodom Sihanouk, there was grave danger that they would follow him into day-to-day political squabbling. Conscious of this danger, I later had an opportunity of asking Prince Sihanouk what he thought. He replied categorically that Cambodian Buddhist monks must not support or take part in the activities of a political party. He did, however, admit that in the course of increasing their knowledge, consciously or unconsciously, they were learning to take an interest in politics. The Buddhist monks of Ceylon, and to a less extent those of Burma, are notorious for the part they play in local politics, though what this has to do with Buddhism is hard to say. I asked myself why the Cambodian monks were different, and found at least part of the answer. When the British took possession of Ceylon and captured the old capital, Kandy, at the beginning of the nineteenth century, they abolished the Kandyan monarchy. When at the end of the century they annexed Upper Burma and captured Mandalay, they deposed the Burman kings. By contrast, Cambodia was allowed by the French to keep her monarchy, and today boasts that her Buddhist monks are disengaged from politics. How long this situation will remain is uncertain, but it could change overnight if Prince Sihanouk allowed the Buddhist hierarchy to become identified with one political party, instead of remaining what it is at the time of writing, the common heritage of all Cambodians, the means whereby each and every citizen can acquire Buddhist merit.

CHAPTER TWENTY-TWO

FULL MOON AT PRAH KHAN

Early the next afternoon we were walking alongside the outer walls of the great Khmer temple of Prah Khan. This I knew was a place where many traces of the ancient Khmer road from Angkor can be found. The temple of Prah Khan was one of the three huge citadels built by Jayavarman the Seventh outside Angkor itself. On the road ahead, between Prah Khan and Angkor, we would pass another of these citadels, called Beng Mealea. Measured along its outer enclosure, Prah Khan is more than three times the size of Angkor Wat, and nearly twice the size of the ancient Khmer capital, Angkor the Great. It is almost a city in itself, and there were once many buildings within its walls. If you superimposed the north-east corner of Prah Khan on Hyde Park Corner, London, the north-west corner would touch the traffic jam at Shepherd's Bush. The south-east corner would be on Clapham Common, and the south-west corner in Putney. If you put Prah Khan down in New York, it would almost cover Brooklyn. As we stood on the threshold of this great Khmer monument, I still had no evidence that an ancient Khmer road once ran eastwards from here to Binh-Dinh. I knew no more than when I set out.

We plodded through the long grasses. The cart-track suddenly led into the outer eastern gate of Prah Khan. The rickety-looking triangular opening above our heads reminded me that the Khmer architects never learnt how to build an arch. They just piled up overlapping stones till they met at the top. There are no keystones, as we know them. Looking through the grass to see

194

when we would come to the main sanctuary, my eye was caught by a smaller building on the right, to the north of our path. I recognized what it was with excitement, an ancient Khmer rest-house, intact except for its western tower. On the north side it was enclosed by bushes, and on the south by long grass.

The building before our eyes once formed the sanctuary of a rest-house. The actual sleeping-quarters, probably made of wood, have long since disappeared. It was possible to push through the long grass and enter by the original entrance into a small portico on the east side. The long central chamber was enclosed on the north side by a solid wall. There were four square windows on the south. Two of these windows were blocked by termite hills. The two central windows were open. The window near the west still had six of its prison-like stone bars. Perhaps it is these bars which have suggested the name 'prison' which the modern Cambodians give this building, since they have long forgotten its original purpose. Coming from Champa, this would be the traveller's first impression of the ancient Khmer empire, a resting-place for weary pilgrims, evidence of a great king's pious concern for his subjects. Where the broken masonry lay in heaps, Buddha, the healer, kept watch no more. There was no living thing near the ancient sanctuary except the industrious termites.

Grass was head high. We continued our way southwards along a narrow path, which led to the inner gate of Prah Khan. The central courtyard beyond lay behind a huge heap of fallen masonry tangled with jungle plants. The temple of Prah Khan is still a total ruin, and has not, like Angkor, been restored by the French. However, parts of its inner courtyard were clear of grass and undergrowth. This clearance work was done by a group of Cambodian pilgrims from nearby villages, who gave their services free as an act of piety for the 2,500th Anniversary of the Buddhist

Era. Near the north-east corner of the inner courtyard there was a pool where the water was clear and could easily be drawn for drinking. The courtyard itself was dotted with tumbled Khmer towers. The sculptures, now held in the grip of giant rain-trees, were roughly hewn. This is a characteristic of late Khmer sculpture, especially the reign of Jayavarman the Seventh, in which many temples were begun and many left unfinished.

Near the north-west corner there was a wooden *sala* open on its north side, and some wooden huts where old women practised meditation. Wayside travellers had told me in advance about the kind of meditation we could expect to find being practised at Prah Khan. The object of this meditation was to catch sight of Nirvana, the Buddhist paradise, or one of the many other Cambodian paradises. I have often discussed paradise with Cambodian peasants. They believe that Nirvana is peopled with beautiful goddesses, whom they call *tevodas*. These female deities minister to the saved. One of my friends, a corporal in the Cambodian Army, once expressed a wish in my presence that at least a few of the deities in paradise ought to be Viet-Namese. Cambodians have a dark brown skin, which they describe in their own language as 'black'. The Viet-Namese have a pale skin, which makes the female of their species attractive to the Cambodian male. At the risk of labouring the point, the Cambodians are *not* black. They are brown. Because they wish their skin was lighter than it is, they describe themselves with a word which means 'black'.

The old women at Prah Khan used to start meditating after dusk, and continue till just before dawn. Then there would be a short break for a meal. Meditation used to start again at half-past seven and continue till late afternoon. They concentrated their thoughts on sticks of incense, fat ones burning for three or four hours without a stop. Or else they would look at circles cut in the wall of a hut, or a colour, or a statue of Buddha. One woman in every fourteen would catch a glimpse of Paradise, the wayside travellers had told me. There are two schools of meditation in Cambodia – the monks, who do very little meditation themselves and disapprove of 'forgetting the body', and certain independent-minded laymen, who strive to 'forget the body' during meditation, and sometimes succeed. At the time of my visit to Prah Khan the meditators were reduced to one Buddhist monk, two old women, and a little girl. The girl had conjunctivitis, which I tried to cure with some ointment. One of the old women saw yellow matter sticking to the child's eyes, and before I could stop her wiped the ointment off. The girl cried. The two old women were sweeping leaves, carrying water, and cooking food. One of them explained that looking after even one Buddhist monk meant a lot of work. When there were more people to help her she spent much time in meditation, and used to see Nirvana, or one of the Paradises, once a month.

'What is it like?' I asked.

'Light,' she replied, looking upwards into the rain-forest. 'Light shining at me very bright, very dazzling.'

She had these glimpses at night-time. Then she told me about the monk – the only Buddhist monk living at Prah Khan, which is not itself a Buddhist monastery but only the ruins of an ancient Khmer temple. The monk, it seemed, was an odd fellow. He did not belong to the monastery in the neighbouring village, but had wandered all over this region looking for a good place to meditate. Prah Khan was ideal for his purpose, though he found it rather quiet, and, if he had some money, would like to make a trip to the Cambodian capital. Near to the ruins of three ancient Khmer towers, the monk had prepared a runway where he walked up and down practising meditation. From a hut in the corner of the courtyard a beaten-earth path led some eighty paces along the base of the northern wall. At both ends of the runway there were little beaten-earth roundabouts which enabled the meditator to turn on his tracks and walk continually without having to negotiate any difficult corners. At one end there was a stone Buddha. This area round the monk's runway was littered with *baysei* which had been brought and offered to Buddha by villagers on previous feast-days. The *baysei* is made from the trunk of a banana-tree and is decorated with chaplets of leaves sewn together with thread. Its purpose and origin is obscure. The Cambodians have many customs which do not seem to be purely Buddhist in their origin, but either come from Hindu practices which they once followed in the days of Angkor or spring from animist worship of local spirits. The stone phallus, Hindu symbol of Siva, can be seen decorating the approaches to many an ancient Khmer temple. Since the *baysei* is the same shape, it is tempting to find some connection. I have seen huge man-sized *baysei* used at the ordination ceremony of Buddhist monks, sometimes wrapped in cloth, perhaps suggesting that in some way the *baysei* symbolizes the novice's renunciation of life as he takes the yellow robe of the Buddhist monk.

After talking to the old women of Prah Khan I knelt down before the Buddhist monk, and offered him the traditional alms of tea, incense, and tobacco. Shaking hands with a Buddhist monk is taboo. Those monks who know western ways shake hands as a matter of politeness, but to a Cambodian peasant this seems shocking. Today was the day of the full moon, as I saw from my calendar. In the evening we saw it rise over the eastern gate of Prah Khan, then it went up quickly into a fretwork of giant rain-tree branches. Monkeys clattered from tree-top to tree-top.

My thoughts turned to Buddhism. Was this close contact with monks and monasteries leading to a belief in Buddha and the supposed merit acquired from Buddhist alms-giving? Looking back now, I can say 'No' definitely, but at this point on the journey it was hard to discount the atmosphere of Prah Khan and its inmates. One of the old women came walking through the ruins, her head shaven. I noticed she wore all-white garments, from which I knew she was observing the precepts of Buddha on this day of the full moon. One of these precepts ordained that she should fast after midday, and for some reason or other I followed her example. 'Ah, yes,' she said knowingly, 'I never eat myself after midday on the day of the full moon.' According to the Buddhist tradition of Cambodia, laity must observe at least eight of the ten Buddhist precepts on holy days like the day of the Full Moon.

These are the ten Buddhist precepts.

(A) *Five Precepts which must be obeyed by all laity every day.*
  1. Do not take life.
  2. Do not steal.
  3. Do not commit sin against virtue.
  4. Do not lie.
  5. Do not drink alcoholic drinks.

(B) *Three more precepts optional for laity except on holy days.*
  6. Do not eat after the regular time (i.e. midday).
  7. Do not attend shows which excite the senses, e.g. dancing, singing, and music.
  8. Do not use cosmetics, perfumes, head-dresses, or adorn yourself with flowers.

(C) *Two more optional precepts.*
  9. Do not sit on a high chair, or a luxurious bed.
  10. Do not touch gold or money.

In deference to these Buddhist precepts, the Cambodian Government bans the sale of alcohol throughout the country four times a month, and on other holy days. On these days it is impossible to buy an alcoholic drink except at certain European-style bars, where by a typical gesture of Buddhist tolerance the sale of alcohol is allowed. As far as fasting is concerned, not having to concentrate on the digestion of food certainly helps the mind to think straight, or so I found.

The morning after the full moon the lone Buddhist monk of Phah Khan was bright and cheerful. He explained that he did not like continuous meditation. He would sometimes take a three-day holiday, or else meditate for alternate weeks – seven days on, seven days off.

'My feet get sore from walking up and down,' he said, 'I have to stop sometimes, to let them heal a little.'

Up to this point I had worn a preposterous yellow flower in my bush hat. I wanted to avoid being mistaken for a deserting French soldier. Somehow, the flower made my blue-and-khaki rig-out look less military – anyway, that was the idea. Along the way, especially at Pim's village, there had been all kinds of speculation about the yellow flower, which was artificially made and had been bought in Saigon. The tribesmen and Cambodians enjoyed fingering it, and asking how much it had cost. By this stage the flower was extremely grubby and tousled, so I stowed it deep in my rucksack when we set off the next morning to follow, for the first time, undisputed remains of an ancient Khmer road. This was the known section of the ancient road from Angkor, which I still believe went farther east than Prah Khan, perhaps all the way to the coast, for an inscription says categorically that a road went from Angkor to Champa and had fifty-seven rest-houses along it. A few of these have been found at ten- to fifteen-mile intervals between Angkor and Prah Khan. I had already seen one outside the eastern entrance to Prah Khan, but farther east none have been found. My journey had now lasted six weeks, and the only remaining objective was to reach Angkor, which I estimated would take me another five or six days. Along the way I would see definite traces of the ancient road, but would not be adding anything new to what is already known about it.

CHAPTER TWENTY-THREE

BUPP

We left Prah Khan by the western gate. The grass was still head-high, and there was no sign that any motor vehicle had been that way for a very long time. The monk said he had seen none since taking up residence earlier in the year. This was the ancient Khmer road all right. From time to time, as the modern cart-track twisted through the trees, the old road came into view, terraced above the surrounding brushwood. Then came the ancient Khmer bridges. By the end of the day we had seen four stone bridges, two of which still served the modern cart-track. The other two lay north and south of the track respectively. To call the track 'modern' is to endow it with qualities which it did not have. One or two wooden bridges served it near Prah Khan. Elsewhere, it descended into the beds of intersecting streams and climbed lazily up beyond. The old Khmer road ran high above the flood.

Twelve kilometres from the outer limit of Prah Khan we crossed an ancient Khmer bridge nineteen feet wide and twenty-three feet long. The stream beneath was very shallow. Scholars have wondered why the ancient Khmer engineers built bridges over small streams and ignored larger watercourses in the same region. An answer often given is that bridges, like all the buildings of Jayavarman the Seventh, were planned at top speed, and some of them never finished. There is something in this argument, but it is not the whole story. Where an ancient Khmer bridge crosses what today seems an insignificant little stream, there is sometimes a big stream a little farther down the road. The big stream need only have changed its course, and the problem of a missing bridge is solved. The problem is not entirely solved, because there are important streams near which no relics of an ancient Khmer bridge have been found at all, and which seem to have been forgotten by the builders for reasons unknown.

During the afternoon we passed the site of Trouvé's rest-house. It was built as a convenient halting-point between Prah Khan and the rest-house down the road. The modern village which formerly lay south of the route near here has been abandoned. This means that the modern traveller has to make a forced march from Prah Khan to the next village without having anywhere to stop on the way – more than twenty miles. In the time of the ancient Khmer empire there was a rest-house, which was discovered by Trouvé. Georges Alexandre Trouvé was a chubby-faced young architect, who had a special talent for 'finding' things. Since his name was 'Trouvé', this was most appropriate. Another French scholar said about him: 'He had a real flair for archaeology, which made him start excavating at the very place where a stele would be buried whose existence he only guessed at.' Trouvé's greatest finds came after he discovered that treasure-wells existed in the bowels of certain ancient Khmer buildings. He developed his own methods of excavation, and unearthed relics of a huge Buddhist statue from no less a temple than the Bayon, that monument made of Buddha-heads. The discovery was celebrated with public rejoicing round the Bayon, at which the King of Cambodia presided. Two months later Trouvé committed suicide, a tragic death which deprived the French of a brilliant young architect. He was only thirty-three, younger even than Henri Mouhot at the time of his death. It was typical that Trouvé should have found an unknown rest-house on the ancient road to Champa years after others had given up the search.

A rest-house on the
ancient road

The great stone bridge of
Ta-Ong

At the next village I repeated my usual questions about Angkor. I was now told that Angkor Wat was built by certain mythical kings. The people also knew a legend according to which a goddess had been sent to do the building by Indra, one of the gods in the Hindu pantheon. My informants had never been to Angkor themselves.

'Why not?' I asked.

'I have no relations there,' said one of them, 'I am afraid the Government will arrest me when they see I am a stranger without any family.'

There were no grounds for such fear, and indeed the Cambodian police, especially at Angkor, would be more than busy if this was their criterion for arresting people.

The next day we crossed two more ancient Khmer bridges and then came to another of Jayavarman the Seventh's rest-houses. It had the unmistakable characteristics which enable one to identify this kind of building. The east entrance was blocked, but the west tower was open. The little room beneath measured sixteen feet wide and eight feet long. The whole building was surrounded by a rambling red wisteria, for which my guides did not know the Cambodian name. On we went through the forest. Suddenly a military truck came up from behind and stopped alongside. There were a few Cambodians aboard, led by an unshaven American. It was the first vehicle we had seen for many days. The American was part of a mission which was in process of photographing the whole of Cambodia by air. The U.S.A. had already financed a similar project in Thailand. Angkor itself has often been photographed from the air, and the results give interesting information on ancient Khmer irrigation systems. I had been warned before setting out that aerial photography was the best method of finding unknown traces of the ancient road to

Champa. After failing in my search, it was encouraging to learn that aerial photographs of Cambodia will soon be available for further study. We were pleased to shake this American by the hand and wish him good luck on his mission. By midday we reached the most enduring part of the ancient road to Champa, the great stone bridge of Ta-Ong, with its arches tapering high above the water. After seven hundred years it was still in use, and had just carried the weight of a heavy U.S.A. truck belonging to the American with whom we had been speaking. I could not help comparing this ancient Khmer bridge with the French colonial bridge over the Sre Pok, so fine and so short-lived.

Mention of a truck shows that we were now very close to Angkor and the outside world. If my journey appears to have been difficult in any way, it was only because I had chosen to make this particular journey in this way. I would not like to give the impression that all of Cambodia is remote and difficult to reach. On the contrary, there is an airfield at Angkor, which you can reach from London in about two days or in even less time if you go by Paris. Aeroplanes arrive daily from the west (Bangkok), and east (Saigon). There are also planes to and from Phnom Penh, the Cambodian capital, which stands on the River Mekong and has a distinct charm of its own. The chief attraction for tourists is the *Fête des Eaux,* a three-day festival of boat-races in honour of the Cambodian King. It takes place in the autumn and marks the moment when flood-water ceases to flow backwards up to the Great Lake, and turns seawards down to the delta of the River Mekong. The Royal Cambodian Ballet performs privately inside the Royal Palace, but there are sometimes opportunities of seeing public performances. There are good hotels and tourist facilities, both in Phnom Penh and at Angkor. The Cambodian Government has made great efforts to attract tourists, especially to Angkor. Tourist visas can be obtained quickly in Bangkok, from where there are properly organized tours to Angkor and return. These tours are suitable for the elderly and frail as well as for the young and adventurous. One old lady, an American I think, saw Angkor, and expressed a dying wish in the U.S.A. that her ashes be flown back to Cambodia and scattered among the ruins of the ancient Khmer capital. This is the kind of bewitching effect which Angkor has long exercised over those who once set eyes on the ruins.

My own journey was off the beaten track, and I had to rely on the help of guides, more than one hundred of them. I preferred to call them companions, for they never acted as porters, though often offered to help carry some of my impedimenta. All through Cambodia, especially, we had raised each other's spirits with talk and joking. Each new guide had different questions to ask, reacted differently to our surroundings, and differed from his predecessor in attitude to life and our journey. They had pleasant little customs, such as hanging up the remains of our daily banana-leaf-wrapped lunch packet on some tree-bough over-looking the path. 'If a hungry traveller comes,' they said, 'here is good rice for him. We learned this custom from the Buddhist monks.' There was a good deal of speculation as to who I might be, and only occasionally did I meet anyone who could talk intel-ligibly about the ancient Khmer civilization. Then the villagers would speak excitedly, while one of them explained with gran-diloquent gestures about the fame and fortune which would attend my discoveries. But what pleased me most was the oft-repeated asides, not really intended for my hearing, but which I often heard. 'He's just like us,' they used to say. 'He knows about ploughing, and sowing, and making rice-cakes for Buddhist festi-vals. He speaks properly to monks, and goes to monasteries on holy days' – not strictly true – 'you should hear him speak "culture" words. He knows more "culture" words than us. He knows "independence", "neutrality", and how to speak to kings and princes. He knows how to say "under the dust of Your Majesty's feet", but he hasn't got a wife. His sister has three children, and his brother is going to get married next month. He's in a hurry to get back to his home village and worship the flower of the betel-palm at his brother's wedding.' However long or short the conversation; it usually ended like this.

'Do you miss your home country and your family?' and 'Will you miss *srok khmer* (Cambodia) when you've gone?'

To both these questions I answered, 'Yes.'

One day I shocked the guides by hanging up a pair of trousers on a peg and lying down to sleep underneath. I was committing what the Cambodians call *bupp*, a mixture of sin and bad luck. When a child goes to sleep on a bed higher than his parents in the same room, this is *bupp*. A layman who enters a monk's cell without removing his shoes commits *bupp*. So it is *bupp* to let a pair of empty trousers hang above the heads of recumbent humans. Perhaps I ought to mention that I had only one pair of trousers and that, whenever we rested or stopped for the night, I changed into a sarong, a length of cloth which you wrap round yourself or step into if it is sewn into a tubular shape. My sarong stretched from the navel down to the ground. Most Cambodians wear a sampot, which is shorter, and hangs to just below the knees. When the Cambodian takes a bath, and I did it the same way throughout my journey, he stands in front of the house wearing a sampot, which he tucks between his legs and fastens at the base of the spine. Then he takes a small silver or brass bowl, or in poorer houses the shell of a coconut, and pours water over his head. When he has finished washing, he puts on a dry piece of cloth over the wet one, then pulls away the wet one from underneath with a brisk tug and lets it fall to the ground. The women do the same, using the cloth in a slightly different way so that it covers their breasts but leaves the thighs more exposed. I was so 'Cambodianized' in all these matters that cordial relations were invariably established with my hosts and guides. They were not above trying to pull my leg by pretending that *bupp* had limitless applications. For example, in one village, there were two monasteries. When I said I was going to visit the monastery on the north side of the village, one wag said that this was *bupp,* and I must visit the monastery on the west side first. When he realized I knew he was having me on, there was a chorus of approval from the other villagers, and a good deal of laughter.

CHAPTER TWENTY-FOUR

THE 'ÉCOLE FRANÇAISE'

The next morning our party was seven strong. It included two *chivapols* carrying venerable firearms, a woman with a bundle of silk skirts, and the village headman on a tiny Cambodian horse. It would not be strong enough to carry him to his destination and back, so he led another horse on a halter. After an hour and a half the modern cart-track turned away to the south. Westward lay an excellent piece of the ancient Khmer road along the banks of a stream known as the Little Elephant stream. The terracing of the ancient road was easily distinguishable in the bushes. The branches of young trees joined over our heads. There was just room to pass in single file. The sun was shut out from overhead.

There could be no better prelude to arriving at Angkor than Beng Mealea, another of Jayavarman's provincial towns like Prah Khan, but one on which the French have already started the work of restoration. By the French I mean the French School of the Far East, known as the E.F.E.O., which stands for *École Française d'Extrême Orient*. The work going on at Beng Mealea is what they call *dégagement et anastylose* – that is clearing the jungle and rebuilding the ruins stone by stone.

The head of the French camp at Beng Mealea was a young architect. For more than a year he had lived in this remote corner of the forest with his wife and three blonde daughters. He knew I was on the way. Judge our disappointment when we marched out of the forest and found the French camp deserted. As there was nobody to show us round, I set off to find the ancient Khmer rest-house by myself. I met some Buddhist monks, to whom I described the kind of building I was expecting to find. They understood, and led me to a familiar-looking Khmer monument, partly in ruins. It lay on the west side of Beng Mealea, so a traveller coming from Champa would have to pass the main buildings of Beng Mealea before reaching it. At Prah Khan it had been the opposite – the rest-house on the Champa side, that is the east side of the main buildings. Beng Mealea is a tumbled chaos of ruins like Prah Khan, except where the French have been at work.

French occupation of Indo-China was scarcely a golden age, but one bright light shone in the centre. Though France generally failed to find men capable of following in the footsteps of the pioneers, one department succeeded – the personnel of E.F.E.O. Not only was there an unbroken succession of brilliant men, but in less than fifty years after its creation the school had produced so many scholars that it is now reckoned to be the equal of any such institution throughout the world. Henri Marchal is typical of the kind of men who work for the French School at Angkor. Now a white-haired old man in his eighties, he is known by some as 'The Father of Angkor'. His lifetime has spanned the *travaux* of the French School at Angkor. In retirement he has chosen to spend his last days in a house beside the Angkor river.

The French School's work, and by definition Marchal's, can be divided into three epochs. The first, from 1908 till 1930, was spent on clearing the jungle, discovering new ruins, and the construction of roads. These roads now permit tourists to see the more important ruins, such as Angkor Wat, and the Bayon, by car. The second epoch lasted till 1942, the reconstruction period, with Marchal in charge much of the time, assisted by Trouvé and others. The third period lasted from 1942 till the early fifties. Political troubles and insecurity prevented the French School from carrying out its full programme. Buildings which were thought safe began collapsing, including Angkor Wat itself in 1947. Characteristically, it was Marchal, already an old man, who came to the rescue.

When Arnold Toynbee wrote about Angkor in *The Observer*, he called it 'A Foretaste of Nirvana', saying that 'one could spend the rest of one's life sitting there'. One could, and Marchal does. He lives on happily in the shadow of the great temple which has shaped his life. When he reaches his hundredth year he may reflect sadly that few of the French pioneers lived to die in their beds. Many, like Henri Mouhot and Georges Trouvé, died suddenly in their thirties. Visitors to Cambodia should not fail to have a talk with this gracious Father of Angkor, as legendary now as the great temples he has helped to rebuild. The reconstruction of Angkor has always been directed by the French, thus fulfilling an old Cambodian prophecy told to a missionary in the seventeenth century:

> 'There are in Cambodia he writes the ruins of an old city which some say was constructed by the Romans or Alexander the Great. The pagans preserve a tradition that this city is destined to be rebuilt by foreigners.'

Foreigners were destined to rebuild Angkor, says the prophecy, and the French are doing the job most handsomely. There were no signs of their building squads at Beng Mealea, so I stayed the night with the village headman, who kindly accompanied me the next day on a walk which would bring me to within a few miles of Angkor itself.

The first landmark to come into view was a wart-like hill north of the path. One of the four hills of Angkor, it is like Mount Lycabettus at Athens, conspicuous but unimportant. Looking back towards the east, we could see the barn-like form of another hill, much larger. Beng Mealea lies at its foot, but the previous day we had been too close underneath to see it. The stones which built Angkor came from this hill, probably by water, and the Angkor river rises in its rocky forests. Just outside the walls of Angkor the Great there is a very small hill, the Phnom Bakheng, whose slope and summit were used, like the Acropolis at Athens, to build important monuments, especially in the tenth century A.D. There is a fourth hill, which lies on the edge of the Great Lake, south of Angkor Wat. This is probably where the Chams disembarked when they sailed up the Mekong to sack Angkor in 1177.

We were carrying an open tin of condensed milk, in which ants insisted on drowning themselves in strict defiance of Buddhist precepts. I pointed this out to my companion, who said that it was wrong to kill insects, including flies and mosquitoes. At midday we met a group of Buddhist monks chopping wood to build a new *sala*. They asked where I was going.

'Angkor the Great,' I replied.

Then one of them asked me: 'Why are you making your journey alone?' This was a fair question. Though I had always travelled with guides, I was the only one who had come all the way from the coast. The question was easy to answer.

'Well,' I said. 'I asked a Cambodian friend to come with me, but he didn't accept the invitation.'

'Why not?' asked the monks.

'He was Cambodian,' I explained, 'like you, Venerables. His home was in Cambodia, but my journey started in Viet-Nam.

'*Yuan* country?' inquired the monks.

'Yes,' I went on. 'You see, my friend didn't trust the Yuan. He said they were a bad lot, and if he had the choice, he would rather keep his feet off Yuan soil.'

That is what the Cambodians call the Viet-Namese – the 'Yuan', or men from Yunnan in South China. One thing the Viet-Namese dislike intensely is being called 'Yuan' by the Cambodians. It irritates them in the same way as being called 'Annamite' by the French – shades of a colonial past. Leaving the monks at work on their *sala*, we walked along a sandy track till late in the afternoon. Dust flew up from water-buffaloes' hooves as a young Cambodian herdsman drove them back to his village. The sun began to go down and came at us anglewise west-south-west. Its last red rays lit up the leaves of sugar-palms dimly seen in a fog of dust. The stretch of the ancient Khmer highway was never so straight as here. Once we crossed a stone bridge. Its balustrades were hidden in the bushes, but we parted the branches to reveal the sculptured faces of a nine-headed snake. According to Cambodian legend, the Khmers were descended from a Hindu prince who married a snake-princess. There was once a gold tower inside the royal palace of Angkor the Great, where a serpent-spirit with nine heads was said to live. The spirit used to appear to the Khmer king disguised as a woman, and the king had to sleep with her every night before he joined his wives and concubines in another part of the palace. In this way the royal stock of the Khmers was perpetuated. If the king missed even one night his death-warrant was as good as signed.

Now the sun was almost setting. Rising dust hid a caravan of Cambodian ox-carts as they lumbered and creaked towards the ancient city of the Khmers. We stopped in a village for the night. 'Did our people really build Angkor the Great?' said one of the villagers. 'Look at us now. Was it possible?' These lovable and carefree Cambodian peasants could hardly believe they were descended from the builders of Angkor Wat and Angkor the Great. I was thirsty after a long day's walk, so they gave me

We parted the branches to reveal the sculptured faces

two ripe coconuts, whose juice I sipped quietly in the twilight. The next morning I hoped to reach Angkor, and wondered if at this eleventh hour something would happen to prevent my completing the journey. The room of the rice-farmer's house where I slept was shuttered, so at first I did not see the dawn when it came. Into this closed room crept a firefly. First it flew round the roof, then up and down the walls. It must have entered by a crack in the floorboards. According to Cambodian tradition, when a firefly enters a Buddhist monk's cell during the night it means that, in the morning, laymen will come to the monastery and give a child to the monks for education. The child is a gift of the laity. As long as he is living in the monastery, his monk-teacher is absolute lord and master. If a firefly enters a room of a layman, Cambodians say: 'The firefly brings news.' There is also a debased form of the proverb which says that when flies buzz round a room they also bring news. Perhaps this is why two of Cambodia's daily newspapers have offices near the central market of the capital. The firefly came just before dawn. What news did he bring, I wondered? Signs and portents – were they as preposterous then as they seemed afterwards from the security of a May morning in England?

I wondered what sort of a man was Jayavarman the Seventh. It has been suggested that the smiling Buddha-faces of the Bayon give us a life-like portrait of Jayavarman himself. He came to the throne late in life, marching from a provincial command in Champa to claim his royal inheritance at Angkor. When he reached Angkor he had to bide his time before overthrowing a usurper. He was a religious man who felt deeply for the sufferings of his people. We learn this from a twelfth-century inscription which tells of the great king's compassion for his subjects. Besides building roads and rest-houses, he established many of the hundred and two hospitals which ministered to sick and suffering throughout the ancient Khmer empire. 'He suffered from the illnesses of his subjects,' says the inscription, 'more than his own; for it is the public grief which makes the grief of kings, and not their own. Full of sympathy for the good of the world, the king expressed this wish as well: "All beings who are plunged in the ocean of existence, may I rescue them from it by the merit of these good works."' As for Jayavarman's march from Champa, I wondered if he climbed up to the plateau on a white elephant, or did he ride a tiny Cambodian horse and lead another by the halter as he went? Did he sleep under trees or in houses? What were his thoughts when he looked back on Champa and every day's march brought him nearer home to Angkor? He thought, maybe, that one day he would send his stonemasons and engineers to build a road, encouragement for the merchant, welcome for the traveller, and inspiration to the pilgrim.

CHAPTER TWENTY-FIVE

ANGKOR THE GREAT

I said good-bye to my host, a swarthy Cambodian farmer, who wished me good luck on this the last day of my journey from the coast to Angkor. He sent two villagers with me to act as guides. I remember that like previous guides, they wished to carry on an animated conversation, but I was not in the mood. Just over an hour's walk brought us to the end of our sandy track and out on to a tarmac road, where stately ruins of Khmer temples peered at us silently through the trees. This was the first glimpse of my journey's end. Our final destination was the Bayon, that temple of Buddha-faces in the centre of Angkor the Great. But the sight of a tarmac road and these first temples on the outskirts made me realize suddenly that I had reached Angkor, and very shortly my journey would be over. I remember very clearly my thoughts at this moment. They were thoughts of another journey, another road to Angkor. I could see myself in distant Thailand at the northern extremity of a road which once led north-west from Angkor the Great. From there I imagined myself moving south-east towards the Dangrek hills and the Thai–Cambodian frontier. I could hardly wait for the moment when I might travel to the north-west extremity of this road, and begin to trace its many stone bridges and rest-houses all the way from the hills of Thailand to Angkor the Great.

Another hour's walk along the tarmac road brought us to the ancient Khmer bridge which once carried the road to Prah Khan across the Angkor river. There is a modern bridge alongside it

A young Cambodian

today, for the river has changed its course over the centuries. We could now choose by which gate to enter the city of Angkor the Great. Due east from the Bayon lies the Gate of the Dead, unrestored by the French and approachable from the east only by an overgrown forest track. North-east of the Bayon, also in the eastern wall of the ruined city, there is a second entrance, called the Victory Gate. Soon we were looking at its giant face, of Buddha, the healer, framed between tree-tops against a blue sky. On either side of our highway, statues of gods and demons, more than life-size, tugged at the stone bodies of familiar Naga snakes. The outstretched snakes formed the parapets to the left and right, which disappeared into the gateway of stone. On the gateway itself were sculptured elephant heads with long hanging trunks nibbling stone lotuses. The guides looked approvingly as I doffed my dusty bush-hat, then all three of us together passed beneath the giant face of Buddha, and entered the ruined city.

The road took us past more Khmer temples and on into the heart of Angkor the Great. Already visible at the end of an avenue of towering rain-trees, stood the ruins of Jayavarman's royal palace. A frieze surrounded the entrance staircase – elephants marching in stone, and mythical birds called garudas holding the balustrades in their upraised claws. The sky was a powerful blue. Monkeys raced through the tree-tops. But the Royal Palace was not the end of our journey. Turning southwards, we caught a first glimpse of the Bayon. As we approached, its huge stone faces received us in silence. The exhilaration of arriving safely, which was enough to make me forget like a good traveller the difficulties of the journey, was double for me, because this was Angkor, not only Angkor the Great and Angkor Wat, but many other ruined temples holding for me many other memories. As we looked in silent wonder at the smiling faces of the Bayon, the sun above was hidden for a moment behind a cloud. But not the moon, which hovered high in the western sky, a pale thing in daylight compared with the full moon which I had seen rise over the eastern gate of Prah Khan. The guides smiled. We threw down the baggage in a dusty heap – a tattered sleeping-mat, rucksack, bow and arrow from Pim's village, the sabre, and most important of all the motorcar-tyre sandals which had brought me safely all the way from Binh-Dinh. The journey was over.

I might at this point embark on an account of the beauties and majesties of Angkor, but there is something about these great

The ancient road between Beng Mealea and Angkor

ruins which makes people shy of describing them. Perhaps the best method is banality. Who could improve on Lord Northcliffe's remarks when he went to Cambodia as a reporter for his newspaper? 'No Sultan', he cabled, 'no Mikado, no Viceroy of India could offer his guests a comparable spectacle.' Or one can view Angkor from afar like the Indian poet, Rabindranath Tagore: 'To know my country in truth (he writes) one has to travel to that age when she realised her soul and thus transcended her physical boundaries.' To know India one has to arrive at Angkor first. Sir

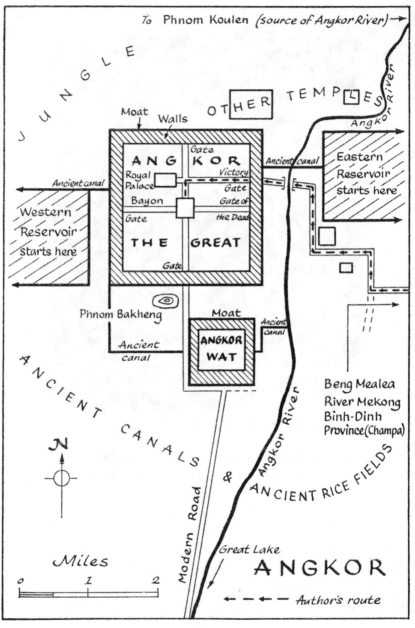

Fig. 2: Angkor the Great is a City; Angkor Wat is a Temple

Journey's end: the Bayon, Angkor

Osbert Sitwell rates Angkor as 'chief wonder of the world today, one of the summits to which human genius has aspired in stone, infinitely more impressive, lovely, and, as well, romantic, than anything that can be seen in China.' André Malraux writes of Buddhist art as the conquest of immobility. It is this immobile presence of Angkor which smothers the imagination. The traveller receives it in silence and goes his way with sealed lips. To travel a long road is always worth while if a feast awaits the traveller at his destination. Each traveller has to discover Angkor in a

223

different way. For some the best preparation will be a long march through the Cambodian forest, as it was for Henri Mouhot one hundred years ago. Suddenly confronted with Angkor Wat he paused from the journey and noted in his diary that some ancient Michelangelo must have built it. 'It is,' he writes, 'grander than anything left to us by Greece and Rome.'

I had completed my 450-mile trek in seven weeks – three weeks less than I had estimated would be necessary. Though I had successfully visited Pim's village, and later collected a few Neolithic tools, I had failed in my main purpose of finding new traces of the ancient Khmer road from Angkor to the coast. Nevertheless, I derived considerable personal satisfaction from completing the journey on time. This was to be rewarded by an enormous meal, for which I had previously posted a money-order to the *Grand Hôtel d'Angkor*, so that I would be sure of funds to pay the bill. I presented myself at the hotel forthwith.

'*Monsieur*,' said the hotelier sceptically, '*vous voulez … ?*'

'*Je m'excuse*,' I found myself saying, '*Je viens de la brousse*.'

'*Évidemment*,' he replied.

This was civilization once more. He called one of his minions to find me a room. The room was on the wrong side of the hotel – that is the wrong side for seeing Angkor Wat. By opening the door, and opening the door of the room opposite, and opening the veranda doors of the room opposite, I could see several miles out across the rain-forest. High above the trees hovered the five towers of Angkor Wat. I turned the clock back three years to I when I saw Angkor Wat for the first time from this same hotel. My host on that occasion had been a Siamese Prince. Champagne corks popped, and the toast all round was 'Angkor the Great'. This had been my introduction to Angkor, but I could never forget that it was also my introduction to Cambodia.

Turning away from the window, I caught a glimpse of my reflection in the mirror, thinner and dustier than I could ever have imagined possible. Tipping out the contents of my rucksack on the floor, I found among the detritus a crumpled yellow flower and forty-nine sticks of incense. There had been fifty-six originally, of which I gave seven to the Buddhist monk at Prah Khan. Fifty-six was double my age in years. Forty-nine was the number of days spent on the road. Early the next morning, just before sunrise, I left the hotel and made my way to Phnom Bakheng, the small hill outside the walls of Angkor the Great. Half-way up the hill there is a giant footprint, said to be Buddha's. In it I threw the crumpled yellow flower, then continued to the summit, where I lit ten sticks of incense at all four corners of the ruins, and another nine in the centre. Five wisps of smoke curled skywards, matching the five towers of Angkor Wat, which I could see below me in the trees. The silence was broken by a fighter-plane of the Royal Cambodian Air Force, which roared over the rain-forest on a dawn patrol. Its colour was saffron yellow like the robe of a Buddhist monk. Was this a symbol of the new Cambodia, I wondered, rising phoenix-like from the ruins of Angkor the Great?

GLOSSARY

Achar. Teacher, especially village elder officiating at Buddhist ceremonies.

Anastylose. Rebuilding monuments with their original materials. according to the system of construction peculiar to each.

Baysei. Usually a banana trunk stripped of bark and decorated with leaves and incense.

Chivapol. Local defence volunteer (Cambodia).

Jataka. Mythological story about an earlier life of Buddha.

Maison Commune. Communal dwelling in tribal villages of Indo-China.

Montagnarde. Name for tribesmen in the south of Indo-China.

Neak Ta. Local spirits (Cambodia).

Phnom. Hill.

Sala. Wooden shelter for travellers.

Salta Tien. Almshouse for Buddhist Monks.

Sivaita. Devotee of Siva, a deity in the Hindu pantheon.

Terre Rouge. 'Red Earth' found on parts of the Indo-China Plateau.

Tevoda. Cambodian tutelary spirit, roughly equivalent to 'angel'.

Wat. Buddhist monastery or temple.

INDEX

SOLE AGENT BY APPOINTMENT:
FOR THE SALE OF
ORDNANCE MAPS.

Stanfords – A Brief History

1827	Edward Stanford is born to a family of tailors and drapers.
1848	Mr. Trelawney Saunders, an established map and chart store at 6 Charing Cross, employs Stanford.
1853	Stanford becomes sole proprietor of the business, changing the name to Stanfords. Looking to expand his position as the only map seller in London, Stanford takes over the neighbouring premises of 7 and 8 Charing Cross for the shop and acquires premises in Trinity Place for use as a printing works.
1858	The first in the *Stanford's Library Maps* series, *Europe*, is published.
1858	John Bolton joins the business, beginning 67 years of service, during which he is appointed as Chief Cartographer.
1862	Stanfords publishes *The Library Map Of London*. The map is praised by the Royal Geographical Society as "the most perfect map of London that has ever been issued."
1874	The shop moves to 55 Charing Cross. The printing and cartographic works are relocated from Trinity Place to 12-14 Long Acre.
1885	Edward Stanford I retires and his son, Edward Stanford II, takes over the business. Stanfords become sole agents in England and Wales for Ordnance Survey Maps.
1887	*Stanford's London Atlas Of Universal Geography* is published, and is dedicated to Queen Victoria in her Golden Jubilee year.
1893	Edward Stanford II receives a royal warrant as Cartographer to the Queen.
1900	Edward Stanford II enlarges the Long Acre premises to combine the printing and cartographic works with the store, under one roof. By this time notable customers have included Florence Nightingale, General Gordon, Frederick Lugard, John Murray, Ernest Shackleton, Captain Scott and Francis Younghusband.
1901	Edward Stanford II becomes Cartographer to the King.
1902	Sherlock Holmes sends Dr Watson "down to Stanfords" for a map of Dartmoor in *The Hound Of The Baskervilles*.
1904	Edward Stanford I dies.
1914-18	The First World War. Stanfords co-operates with the War Office as a contract publisher.
1917	Edward Stanford II dies. His son, Edward Fraser Stanford takes over the business.
1922	Stanfords produce the smallest maps ever published for a series of minute Atlases for Queen Mary's famous doll's house in Windsor.

Continued on back flyleaf.

EDWARD STANFORD
WHOLESALE & RETAIL MAPSELLER, &c.
12-14 LONG ACRE, COVENT GARDEN, WC